OTHERS SAID NO, BUT GOD SAID YES

THE FAITH JOURNEY OF REV. JOHN L LAMBERT

CHERYL ANN LAMBERT

OTHERS SAID NO, BUT GOD SAID YES
THE FAITH JOURNEY OF REV. JOHN L LAMBERT
By Cheryl Ann Lambert

Book Design: Robert Coalson, rcoalson@netzero.net

Cover Design: Timothy Smith, Perfect Impressions

Published by Substance of Hope Publications
P.O. Box 50973
Indianapolis, IN 46250

ISBN 0-9725780-0-5

Printed in the United States of America

TABLE OF CONTENTS

APPLAUSE FOR

OTHERS SAID NO, BUT GOD SAID YES

"The experiences depicted in the life story of Rev. John L Lambert are in many instances a microcosm of life for the African-American male of his era. The struggles to achieve and overcome adversity are under-girded by a sustaining faith in God and one's own ability. The story of his persistence to overcome the odds against him will be encouragement to those who are presently in a similar struggle. It is refreshing to read of the love and respect a daughter has for her father and mother."

— The Right Reverend Philip R. Cousin
Presiding Bishop – Fourth Episcopal District
African Methodist Episcopal Church

"This is a beautifully written story of a man who was tested by poverty, prejudice and moments of self-doubt. But time and again, he found his strength in family and in faith. As his daughter Cheryl shares her father's life, every page reveals the journey of a man born to serve."

— The Honorable Richard Durbin
United States Senator

"At a time when many young people and especially young African-American males have either not had dreams of what they could become or given up hope on becoming successful leaders, this book is a reminder that dreams still come true when one is willing to work hard, seek God's guidance and listen to the positive voices. In one sense this is a story of Rev. John L Lambert. In another sense it is the story of how a family, a community, the church and an extended family came together to shape, nurture, uplift, encourage and protect a young man and allow him to become a blessing to all who helped him and to the broader community in need of caring, committed leaders.

"*Others Said No, But God Said Yes* will make you laugh, cry, celebrate and remember your own story. It is honest, showing the struggle of real people whose pain you feel. It is above all a story of hope and faith. It is a story of God's creative work of making a man a preacher man. It is a story worth telling and a story worth reading."

— *Dr. Edward Wheeler*
President, Christian Theological Seminary, Indianapolis

"It is better to see a sermon than to hear one. In this life story again and again we see the good news of overcoming. Yes, there are enemies, there is opposition, but there is the helping hand of the Lord. Here is a strong challenge to faith. We thank Rev. John L Lambert for a work in progress through the power of God."

— *Dr. Henderson Davis*
Historiographer (Ret.) African Methodist Episcopal Church

"Ascending the ranks of government to a leadership position is no easy task, especially for African-American males who question authority in a bureaucracy.

"Rev. John L Lambert's story is encouraging and enlightening and an affirmation of faith; a faith that is evidenced by his strong family values, determination to succeed, and his diligence and polite persistence.

"In a time of much negativity and doubt, 'Others Said No, But God Said Yes' is a contemporary reminder of how God works in the every day lives of his people when they commit to him and open their hearts and minds to make their dreams come true."

— *Ms. Audrey McCrimon, Executive, Illinois State Government*

Acknowledgements

The one thing I've always known about my father for as long as I can remember is that he's got my back. And that's more than a notion if you believe everything you hear about preacher's kids.

I remember running in a cross-country meet back in junior high school. Dad was there at the finish line as I was coming in with the final few runners. I overheard him tell one of the other dads: "At least she didn't come in last place."

He had my back.

Years later, when I ran the LaSalle Bank Chicago Marathon, I encouraged him to give a similar response to people who wanted to know how I placed. "What matters is, 2,000 people finished behind her," he'd say. See, to Dad it didn't matter that more than 17,000 runners participated in the marathon that year.

Clearly, he had my back.

And when I got my first real job out on my own, and *inadvertently, accidentally*, charged up a credit card and needed money right away to pay it off…it was Dad who patiently, calmly explained to me how to apply for a short-term, unsecured loan through my local credit union.

Even though he didn't give me the money *that time*, I knew that he still had my back.

Psalm 23:6 says in part: "Surely goodness and mercy shall follow me all the days of my life."[1] I'm just glad that, while my Heavenly Father has my back, my earthly father does, too.

Thanks, Dad.

Cheryl Ann Lambert

FOREWORD

The definition of an angel is probably as varied as there are angels in existence. For me they have simply been agents of God who have done the unscheduled, unplanned, and unexpected to help me along my faith journey.

I have wanted for so many years to tell my story. Over and over I promised myself that one day I would tell my story by writing a book. God knew that depending upon me, it would never get done, so He sent an angel. That angel is none other than our daughter, Cheryl Ann Lambert. I will never be able to find the words to express my gratitude to her. Laying aside as many prejudices as possible, I can truly say that Cheryl Ann took on the task of telling my story as a true professional. She has helped me in the fulfillment of a dream and, at the same time, she has made me so proud. My hope is that others will read this book and come away inspired and encouraged to trust God to make a way even when there seems like there is no way. I also hope it will encourage others to tell their stories.

The completion of this book would not have been possible without other angels. To my wife Martha Ann, whom I love dearly and is my very best friend and who remains angel number one, thank you. To each of my children, Avery, Sharon and family, Bryon, Debbie and family, thank you for beings angels. And again to you, Cheryl Ann, you are in line for special wings. Thank you, my daughter.

Other angels along the way are mentioned at various points in this book. Many are not mentioned simply because the list is too long. More and more angels keep appearing. I'm now convinced that God has an endless supply of them. Thank you to all of my angels. May God ever bless and keep each of you. As you provide angelic service to others, may God ever grant you with your own unlimited supply of angels.

John L Lambert

Prologue

"Where's your lawyer?" the judge asked.

"I couldn't afford one," the man responded.

"Fine," said the judge. "Judgment for the state. Next case."

Startled, the man quickly responded: "But judge, can't I represent myself?"

"Sure," the judge said, as he swiveled his chair around so his back was facing the man. "Go ahead and state your case."

Stunned, the man didn't speak for a moment. When he finally did, he shakily went through his prepared statement, explaining to the judge's turned back that his resources were too limited to pay what the court was requesting. He was too astonished to speak with any eloquence. He stumbled through his statement and drew to an awkward close.

As soon as the man finished talking, the judge turned back around to face him to render the judgment. It was against the man. The judge ruled that he begin immediately making monthly payments to the state of Illinois as required by the Responsible Relatives Act.[2] Illinois state law said that a responsible relative is someone who must pay money to help take care of a family member who receives public assistance. The man's mother had been on welfare for 13 years.

By the time the Illinois State Legislature repealed the Responsible Relatives Act, the man would be in his fifth year of making monthly payments.

Chapter I

Third of Eleven

It was 1967. Heavyweight champion Muhammad Ali had been barred from the ring and stripped of his title for refusing to submit to induction in the armed forces. Julian Bond had finally been sworn in after being denied his seat in the Georgia state legislature for opposing U.S. involvement in the Vietnam War. And Aretha Franklin had just released her hit song, "Respect."[3]

Twenty-five-year-old John L Lambert, husband and father of one son with a new one on the way, was at court in the capital city of Illinois, Springfield. The welfare system that had haunted him since he was a child and an imprudent law in the state had just caught up with him. He'd been summoned to court to begin making payments to the state per the Responsible Relatives Act because his mother, Mildred Lambert, was a recipient of welfare assistance in East St. Louis, Illinois.

John's mother had received public assistance through the Aid to Dependent Children (ADC) beginning in 1954. The state had previously tried to contact several of John's siblings to no avail. When the letters began coming to him, he ignored them for two years. When he got tired of receiving them, he responded explaining his inability to pay. The state's response was a court summons.

"The judicial system is fair and just," John thought at the time. "They'll see that I can't afford to pay."

He'd gone to court armed with copies of his household bills—electricity, insurance, clothing—to prove he didn't have the resources to pay what the court was requesting. Even though he earned more than $400 a month at his first state government job at the Federal Disability Program, an arm of the Department of Rehabilitation Services, he and his wife had only $10 or $20 extra to put toward anything during a given month. His intention had been to state his case that way.

So much for fairness in the judicial system.

* * *

John L Lambert was born and raised in East St. Louis, Illinois, at the time an 80,000-population city next door to St. Louis, Missouri. Throughout his childhood his name had been John L, though the "L" didn't really stand for anything. L was his middle name.

When John L entered the world in 1942, East St. Louis wasn't known for the high poverty rate and depressed job market that low-income residents would face in later years. Quite the opposite, East St. Louis was teeming with black Southern migrants who'd come in search of opportunity in the North. What they found in East St. Louis was a city just decades removed from ranking first in the nation in the sale of horses, mules hogs, processed aluminum, roofing material, paint pigment and coal.

By 1950, more than one-third of the East St. Louis workforce was employed in some form of manufacturing. The largest employer and most visible industry in East St. Louis, the railroads, had been the lifeblood of the city in terms of providing cheap fuel from the Illinois coal mines for the local industries, linking East St. Louis manufacturers with the national market.[4] As a result, the city included all the earmarks of a more metropolitan area: large homes, small homes, housing projects and storefront churches. Black families lived in neighborhood communities, sharing the same schoolyards, stoops and struggles common to any blue-collar culture.

John's family of 10 brothers and sisters—Charles, Freddie Lee, Elmer, Delores, Velma, Alvin, Jerry, Ida, Joyce, and Evelyn—lived in a small yet comfortable home off Collinsville Avenue at 654 North Third Street. Theirs was just one in a row of three blocks of homes. They lived in the city, but could have just as easily been in the country. They had an outhouse (an outdoor toilet housed in a small structure), a smokehouse (a structure in which meat or fish is cured with smoke) chickens, and hogs.

John hated the hogs most of all.

Every year, John's father, Mose, and his father's brother, Uncle Buddy, got together with a neighbor and some of John's brothers to slaughter the hogs. They had the annual ritual down to a science. One man shot the hog, then another split it open to drain. After that, the men would together lower what could be a 300-pound hog into scalding hot water with a pulley and chain. Retrieving the animal, they stripped off its hair and skin to dry it for cooking and curing. The end result was savory sausage, bacon, and ham.

John and his brothers were responsible for daily upkeep of the hogs. That meant finding feed for them. Once a week, he, Charles, Freddie Lee, and Elmer put two or three large canisters into a red wagon. They wheeled the wagon to the closest white neighborhood. There was plenty of food suitable for hogs in the garbage that white families left on the curbside, so John and his brothers picked through each trash can for food waste. The reaction from residents varied from disdain at the boys who were digging through their garbage to delight that their garbage was being emptied at no charge to insistence that the boys take all—not just part—of the trash. They fished out anything edible they could find and put it in their canisters. Once the canisters were full, the Lambert boys wheeled their red wagon back home and put the contents out back for slop in the hog troughs.

The Lamberts didn't have a telephone at home, so they used a pay phone nearby. They didn't have hot water, so they filled a number three tub half with boiling water and half with tap water for bathing. At bath time, John's mother would boil water in several large pots and kettles on their potbellied stove. She continued the arduous task of filling the tub until the water temperature was just right. Her children had a choice: They could either use the same water that an older brother or sister used before them, or they could boil more water and refill the tub again, until the water temperature was just right.

John's favorite thing about growing up was spending time with his maternal grandmother, Mary Dotson. The grandchildren knew her as *Gram*. Gram was a gifted cook who specialized in barbecue and barbecue sauce. She got up early on Saturday mornings in the summer to make her mouthwatering sauce to slather on tender pork ribs. She sold barbecue from her yard from sunup to sundown. No one knew how to make her special barbecue sauce and she shooed anyone away who dared request the recipe.

Gram's cooking ability was only surpassed by her sharp wit. John discovered that the hard way. When she found out he disliked okra, for example, she made a mental note and reminded him of it the next time she cooked for him.

"John L, didn't you tell me you don't like okra?" she asked, pointedly.

"Yes ma'am," he said, finishing up the last satisfying bite of dinner.

"Well, guess what you were just eating?" she asked with a sly smile.

Gram had managed to sneak okra into a mouthwatering meal without John noticing. John was outdone—but not angry. After all, this was the woman who was always in his corner, taking up for him sometimes when he didn't even deserve it. On one such occasion, Gram took up for him following a neighbor's complaint. This particular neighbor was always miffed at John and his brothers and sisters for cutting through her yard on the way to Gram's house. Problem was, the neighbor had a rooster who shared her disdain. The bird flew and clawed at anyone who stepped foot in the yard. John had been attacked by the willful bird many times over. But this time, John was ready for the rooster. He had a stick in his hand.

When the rooster flew towards him, as it always did, John swung hard—hard enough to knock the bird out. A surprised John looked around quickly to see if anyone saw him, then darted off to Gram's. The neighbor came knocking soon afterwards. John hid out in a back room as soon as Gram opened the door, eavesdropping as the woman gave Gram an earful about John. The boy had no business walking in her yard, the neighbor said, and he had no business hurting her rooster. Gram listened and nodded, apologizing and assuring her that John was in serious trouble. No sooner had the door closed behind the neighbor than Gram did an about face. Shaking her head and smirking, she asked herself out loud: How dare that woman complain about her grandbabies walking through her yard when that silly old rooster of hers scratched them all the time?

"John L, you just try to avoid her house when you come over from now on, you hear?" It was the closest John got to being punished that day. Though he had 10 brothers and sisters vying for Gram's attention, he liked to think he was her favorite.

There were no favorites at home—that was obvious by the lavish gifts their father showered on all his children. Mose Lambert worked at the Granite City and Common Wealth Steel Foundries, steel mills in Granite

City, Illinois, 15 miles north of East St. Louis. He earned $250 every other week, good money at the time. He also had a part-time job delivering coal for many of the homes with pot-bellied stoves in the neighborhood.

Mose regularly bought expensive gifts for his children, demonstrating his love through a top-of-the-line B.F. Goodrich bicycle that had handlebar grips and reflector lights, or a Lionel Electric train set complete with box cars, tracks and railroad crossing signals. Mildred Lambert was not impressed. She thought Mose should buy less expensive gifts and put any extra money toward useful household items. The expensive gifts gave the Lambert children bragging rights in the neighborhood, though. Some of the children even turned their noses up at gifts and clothes they got from their church, St. Mark Baptist, at Christmas time. Second-hand gifts were for poor people, they figured, and they weren't poor.

Like any other children in any other neighborhood, the Lambert children and their friends had their share of games and activities to keep them busy. John and Freddie Lee played on the sandlot baseball team under their good-spirited coach, James H. Davidson. John also played basketball at the local Boy's Club of America. A budding athlete, John was recognized early on for his skills. A neighborhood newspaper even published an article about John making five sets of 10 consecutive free-throws during a club-based competition. Given a choice between basketball and baseball; however, John would choose baseball every time.

All of the Lambert children played softball, cork ball (softball with a harder ball), horseshoes and mumblety-peg (a game in which players tossed an ice-pick onto a patch of grass with the object being to make it stick firmly into the ground.) Sometimes they played outside of St. Mark, which was just two doors down. They knocked out many a window playing softball and cork ball in the church lot, to senior pastor Rev. Wings' dismay.

Mose Lambert did not play with his children. Not in the yard for softball or the neighborhood for basketball. That simply wasn't his way. He was a strict man with no-nonsense rules about how his household should operate. All the children were required to call him Daddy until he said they could call him Dad. In addition, he made the boys learn to drive by age 10 or 11 to help out with errands that required driving. Freddie Lee would reminisce later how the boys stacked pillows high in the driver's seat so they could see over the dashboard.

Their father's presence was sometimes a formidable one. In 1952, when John was 10 years old, word came that his father's sister, Alice, had taken ill. She was put into Homer G. Phillips Hospital in St. Louis for extended treatment, and the family visited her every few days. On one particular day, his father decided to have John call to check on her instead of the family going in to visit. Mose gave his son money to use the pay phone that was a block-and-a-half away from home.

When he got to the phone, John dropped his dime in and called the hospital. He asked to speak to Alice Lambert and his call was switched to the nurses' station. The nurse who answered told him his aunt had died that morning. In disbelief, John hung up. He waited a few seconds, took a deep breath, fished another dime out of his pocket, and called back.

"Alice Lambert died this morning," the nurse repeated.

John hung up and ran back home, afraid of what his father's reaction would be. When he got home and told his father the news, Mose Lambert immediately stopped what he was doing. He mumbled something under his breath, stood up, and walked out the front door. John had felt a mixture of sadness and fear at recounting the news. He didn't know how to read his father's reaction.

A year or so later, John and his brother, Freddie Lee, went to their church's revival. Several area churches participated in the service at St. Mark, which traditionally ended once all the people seated at the mourner's bench (a pew reserved up front for newcomers and potential converts) went up front to dedicate their lives to Christ. The mourner's bench was a fixture at any Baptist revival in those days. The revivalist directed the most climactic points of his sermon to those on the mourner's bench as visitors, members and friends spurred him on with claps and shouts. Each night of the revival, one or two people got up from the mourner's bench to make a public confession. Not John. He was the last person left on the bench, and he still didn't go up front that final night.

Just for John, Rev. Wings extended the revival an extra night. John hadn't planned to be the last one on the bench, but he didn't feel ready to go up just yet. He'd been waiting for a feeling, some kind of sign, to go up front. When he still didn't feel anything on that extended night, he decided to get up anyway. As he began to walk up front, he felt a physical and spiritual awakening deep down inside that he knew must be the Holy Spirit. He was happy and relieved as the feeling hit.

At St. Mark Baptist Church, making a public confession for Christ was the first step. The next step was baptism, in which several neighborhood churches got together for a community service. John was looking forward to it. It was a way to prove his manhood with the local boys. Legend had it that if you weren't really born again, you would drown in the baptismal pool. He was eager to prove his faith—especially after all it had taken for him to get up from the mourner's bench.

When John got home to tell his parents about accepting Christ, Mose Lambert became angry. Perhaps Mose was upset because John had made the decision on his own. Perhaps he was upset because he hadn't been there with him during the revival. Whatever the reason, he simply refused to let John be baptized. John was shattered. Fresh in his newfound faith, he did the only thing he thought would do him any good. He decided to pray. He went outside to the back of the house behind the coal-shed (a small wooden structure with a metal roof that kept coal from the elements.) The shed didn't have a floor, instead, coal was piled high off the ground. If he'd been younger, John might have been hiding in the coal-shed. He and his brothers and sisters often played in and around it. Right then, though, he was hiding behind it.

"I've been going to church, and I've been hearing about you, but I don't know if you're really, there," John prayed aloud. "I'm just gonna come out and ask you. Will you please let me be baptized? If you don't, then I'll know you're not God." He turned and walked back into the house.

The following Sunday, an eccentric church mother who was known for talking to herself came over to congratulate John on his upcoming baptism. When John told her he wasn't going to be baptized after all, she became upset. She marched over to talk to John's mother about the situation. The woman was unusually adamant and insistent that John's mother allow him to be baptized. John was surprised. After all, it wasn't every day that the church mother came to his defense.

By mid-week, Mildred and Mose were arguing at home about whether or not John should be baptized. John overheard them, his hopes fading fast. He'd just about given up when he heard his exasperated father's voice. "Okay," said a worn-down Mose. "Just let the boy be baptized."

The meaning of the moment was not lost on John. He knew that God had changed his father's heart and he knew that God had spoken through the church mother. He would never again deny that God was God. He would never again deny that God does answer prayer. He would never again deny that God works in the day-to-day lives of his people.

John witnessed God first-hand later that year when a crisis struck the Lambert family. Their house caught fire. When he got home from Garfield Grade School, John saw the house engulfed in flames. His mother, brothers and sisters were milling around the front lawn, and firemen were spraying the house. His father wasn't home from work by then. All John could do was stand and stare. He watched as a fireman told his mother that no one left inside could be saved. She ignored him. She ran into the fire- and smoke-filled house and emerged with five-year-old Velma in her arms. Her own hair was singed and smoking.

John saw God that day in the courage of his mother

and the survival of his sister. According to the fireman, there was no hope. Mildred Lambert had proved otherwise. Her determination and willful discounting of the fireman's authority left an indelible mark on John. Someone in authority had spoken. He sounded like he knew what he was talking about. He was certain. Yet he was completely wrong.

Once the fire was out, the large family split up to live at three different homes while their house was being repaired. It took weeks before they could move back home. When they did, John harbored a new respect for his mother. But by the time John entered eighth grade at Rock Junior High School, he had a new respect for *the street* as well.

The street could be a dangerous place. A boy needed to protect himself if he didn't belong to a gang. John wasn't in a gang, so he carried a switchblade for protection. He never had to use it, but he let it be known that he had it—just in case. Every morning after he got dressed for school he put the knife in his pocket. Every afternoon when he got home from school, he put the knife in his drawer. One day, though, John forgot to take the switchblade out of his pocket before throwing his clothes in the laundry. His mother found the knife as she was preparing to wash.

Her reaction was worse than the whipping he was expecting. She looked at the switchblade and looked at John with the saddest eyes he'd ever seen. She sighed, brows furrowed, and told him how terrible, dangerous and foolish it was to carry a knife. She talked to him for a long time that day, and John thought for a brief moment that she might cry as she confiscated the knife.

She stated her wishes clearly to John: she never wanted him to carry a switchblade again. She wanted nothing of the street's violence to touch her family, or to become a part of John's life.

John knew his mother had his best interest at heart, but he had the reality of the street in mind. He still needed to protect himself. Less than a month went by before John bought a new switchblade. He carried it with him every day. But he remembered to put it in his drawer after school from that day forward.

CHAPTER 2

Single-Parent Home

In 1954, John began to hear talk among the adults in the neighborhood about the local steel mill. Many of the men who were long-time workers at the Granite City mill were leaving their jobs with cash settlements. Some of them had developed spots on their lungs due to prolonged exposure to the unhealthy work environment. Rumor had it that many steel mill workers weren't sick— they just wanted to get out. If there really was a safety problem at the steel mill, they figured, they'd probably lose their jobs. Why not leave pocketing a little extra cash? Most people even thought the steel mill had a doctor on payroll. When mill workers told their boss they suspected health problems, they were all referred to the same doctor. Anyone who visited the doctor left his office with a report validating any health concern.

Between rumors around town about the mill, John heard his mother and father arguing frequently. He didn't know what the arguments were about at first. Then he overheard his father telling his mother about his decision to request a cash settlement from the steel mill. Their arguments stopped then and for weeks to come. The family waited anxiously for Mose's settlement check.

It was a desperate time for the Lamberts. John's father was unable to find work other than his part-time coal delivery job, and he didn't have any money in savings. It was beginning to seem as though the settlement check would never arrive. Weeks passed, and the limited resources the family had were quickly drying up. Finally, the check arrived. It was a total disappointment when it did. Mose Lambert received a $1,200 settlement, little more than two-and-a-half month's pay. It was a slap in the face after 10 years at the mill.

A few more weeks passed before John's father came to a stark realization: He wasn't going to find another job in or near East St. Louis making mill money. He tried applying for ADC assistance so some money would be coming in, but the agency denied his request. The system didn't make it easy for dual-parent households. He decided to leave home to find work in Indianapolis. Relatives of Mildred Lambert—the kids called them Aunt Searcy and Uncle George even though they were distant cousins—had convinced Mose that there was money to be made in the city.

Indianapolis' convenient proximity—the city is within a day's driving of half the nation's population—had been a boost to its growth as a transportation hub. The city was home to the nation's first union rail depot, Union Station. With the development of the National Road, a steady stream of settlers had poured into Indianapolis during the settlement of the frontier, and it continued to grow year after year.[5] No doubt, Mose could find work in the burgeoning town.

Mildred Lambert was upset when Mose decided to move to Indianapolis. She didn't discuss the situation with her children, but they could tell she was concerned. She thought Mose could have gotten a job in the area, and she told him so. But her husband was accustomed to making a certain amount of money and he was too proud to take a pay cut.

In Indianapolis, John's father found work right away in construction. Once he got settled, he began sending money regularly to his family back in East St. Louis. John thought the family might eventually move to Indianapolis, or that his father might move back home, but it was not to be. In the first few months and years, Mose would come home to visit, and John and some of his brothers would stay with their father in Indianapolis during the summers. It was understood after a time that Mose wasn't coming back home. Mildred and her husband never got a divorce, but theirs became a permanent separation. As time passed, Mose Lambert sent money less and less to the family. After a while, he stopped sending money altogether. The family went through a significant economic transition as a result.

Working outside the home was never an option for Mildred since she was raising six boys and five girls. She decided to contact the welfare office even though the family had been turned down once before. She applied for and was accepted into the ADC assistance program. The once well-fed family found itself eating Spam, commodity cheese and other government-issued foods for the first time.

While the Lambert family struggled through economic issues, blacks in the country struggled through racial issues. In 1955, lynching continued in the South with the brutal slaying of 14-year-old Emmett Till, in Money, Mississippi. *Jet* magazine published a photo of his face, and John saw his mother cry as she looked at the image. That same year, Rosa Parks of the Montgomery, Alabama, chapter of the National Association for the Advancement of Colored People (NAACP), refused to surrender her seat when ordered by a local bus driver. The incident lead to the Montgomery bus boycott of 1955-56.[6]

Though John's world consisted of his home on Third Street, his church two doors down, and his school, the racial tension in the country had an affect on him. He saw how blacks were treated as second-class citizens and he was keenly aware of his family's new socioeconomic position. Somehow, though, the Lamberts managed to keep up appearances. Mildred made sure her children were always neat and clean—and John was no exception. Seeing the clean-cut young John, teachers, neighbors and preachers would often tell him he'd be somebody important one day. Their encouragement planted seeds of perseverance within John's psyche, but he secretly wondered if his encouragers would be as supportive if they knew he was on welfare.

People surely knew the dire financial straits the family was in—John's mother borrowed money from the next door neighbors on occasion—but he worked hard to keep his classmates from discovering his secret. At school, welfare recipients were tagged during registration and got used books after other students got brand new books. John made sure his teacher never found out he was on welfare. It meant he always got a new book just like his better-off classmates.

He even had a system to avoid the mark of welfare when it was time to buy school clothes. Families on welfare got clothing vouchers worth a designated amount of money to spend in select stores. When his mother gave him a voucher to purchase school clothes, John bypassed stores where he could get several off-brand outfits. Instead, he went to Al's Men's World in East St. Louis. It was one of a few retailers that let welfare recipients spend vouchers just like cash on anything in the store.

Welfare recipients were treated as second-class citizens, sometimes even by ADC caseworkers. The Lambert family found this out during one visit from a caseworker. The woman had dropped by the Lambert home because John's mother had requested additional money for a stove repair. She'd requested money for the repair previously, and had been turned down.

The caseworker confronted Mildred Lambert with a barrage of questions about the family's living conditions. She wanted to find out if the Lamberts had any hidden sources of income. The caseworker snapped at John's mother, questioning whether she really needed to get her stove repaired. As if that weren't enough, she refused to give Mildred money for the repair. After she left, John's mother sat down at the kitchen table and began to cry. She had no other means of income.

The incident left an indelible mark on 12-year-old John's mind. To him, his mother was honest and decent, yet the caseworker had all but called her a liar. All Mildred Lambert was trying to do was raise her children to the best of her ability. The interchange hurt John deeply, and his distaste for the welfare system grew. He vowed to one day make enough money to get his family off welfare. Who knew? One day he might even be able to help other families avoid the system altogether.

CHAPTER 3

Not College Material

In a family of 11 children, there are always sibling pairs who are closest to one other. In the Lambert family, John was closest to his oldest brother, Charles. Charles believed in John before John believed in himself, and he always took time out to share advice with his younger brother. Charles had moved to Indianapolis to attend college by the time John entered high school in 1957. He lived with their father. Even long distance, John and Charles' bond remained strong. Charles thought John would make something of himself one day, and he made sure to tell him so. He always encouraged John, and he sent his little brother money when he could. Charles took seriously his responsibility as the first member of the Lambert family to attend college. He encouraged all his brothers and sisters to follow in his footsteps.

The significance of education for black Americans was becoming increasingly clear. In 1957, President Dwight

D. Eisenhower ordered federal troops into Little Rock, Arkansas—400 miles from East St. Louis—after unsuccessfully trying to persuade Arkansas Governor Orval Faubus to give up efforts to block desegregation at Central High School. Three short years later, black college students in Greensboro, North Carolina, launched the sit-in movement by insisting on service at a local segregated lunch counter.[7]

In 1960, Charles was sitting in a college class one day when a professor asked him and his classmates three questions: *Who needs help? Why do you help? How do you help?* The students wrestled with the three questions all semester long, and their professor challenged them to continue pondering them for the rest of their lives. When Charles told John about the questions, John was struck by their magnitude. Though only a high school senior, he decided to accept the questions as a personal challenge, and he vowed to discover their answers.

John's high school, East St. Louis High (East Side) was a predominantly white high school in 1960. A sign of the times, the school had an intense rivalry with all-black Lincoln High School. Blacks made up only 15 percent of the student population at East Side and an even smaller percentage of the faculty. In fact, John's counselor was one of a very few black faculty members at the school. Black or white, though, students at East Side had a healthy rapport with faculty members. That is, with the exception of the boys' basketball and baseball coach, "Pick" Dahner.

It wasn't that Pick wasn't a good coach. In fact, he was known to bring out the best in the East Side Flyers basketball and baseball players. But he was also known for the passion he had for his job that came out in the form of fiery speech and red-faced temper tantrums during ball practice or games. John experienced the coach's temper close-up when he confronted him during basketball season about how the coach never started more than two black players. Coach Dahner exploded. He was offended that John would imply that he or his tactics were racist, and he said so. Repeatedly. Then he turned the tables on John, threatening to start him in the next game so he could put his money where his mouth was. True to his threat, Coach Dahner started John—plus the two other requisite black players—in the next East Side Flyers basketball game. Then he started them in the game after that, and the game after that. Speaking up with the coach had paid off for John. Gradually, Coach Dahner developed a reluctant respect for John's initiative.

John enjoyed being a starting basketball player. To stay sharp, he practiced regularly with the team and took any opportunity to play pickup games. He and his brother, Freddie Lee, were playing basketball at the Lincoln High School gym one afternoon when a tussle erupted between his brother and one of the other players. The problem was, that other player belonged to a gang, and his gang didn't scare easily.

"I'm gonna get you after this game is over," the player said to Freddie Lee, pointing at him and walking off the court.

As the game continued, the boy was lingering on the sidelines, whispering to a group of boys and pointing at Freddie Lee as he did. John and Freddie Lee figured he was telling his friends what happened. They figured right. When the game ended and the two boys stepped outside, at least 15 other boys began to form a circle around them.

Freddie Lee wanted to stay and fight, but John thought running would be their best bet. They were out-numbered, after all. Before either could make a decision, one of the boys closed in and clipped John on the jaw with a slug from the side. It dazed him, and he buckled at the knees. The other boys started to close in too, throwing kicks and punches at him and Freddie Lee. Somehow, they saw a space open up in the group. John and Freddie Lee struggled through the opening and took off running back home, leaving the group of boys behind.

The fight might very well have continued the next day if it hadn't been for a fortunate coincidence. As it happened, one of the gang members who hadn't been outside the gym that day, Bull, lived in the apartment complex where Gram now resided. Bull's father was the apartment's landlord. Bull knew John and Freddie Lee from their visits to see Gram, and he had always been cordial with the boys. Bull squashed the idea of any retaliation when he heard about the fight. He was the toughest of his crew, so his word was final. Thank goodness for friends in high places.

School rivalries and neighborhood disagreements became less important for John as his senior year drew to a close. He had college on his mind by then. Charles had convinced him to go to college, but now John needed some advice about which college to attend. He decided to talk to his counselor about his options. In addition to playing basketball, John had excelled at baseball in high school, but he hadn't gotten a scholarship by then.

Surely his counselor could steer him in the right direction.

"So, what college would you recommend for me?" John asked the counselor as he sat down across from him in his office.

"I really think you should join the military instead of going to college," the counselor suggested.

"But I don't want to do that," John said. "I want to further my education."

"Well, your grades really won't allow you to go to college. If your grades had been higher, then, maybe you could have gone..."

The exchange, which continued for a few more minutes, left John discouraged and confused. Sure, he was an average student who got mostly Cs and a rare A. And true enough, his reading was at one time bad enough that he'd spent a brief semester in a remedial reading class. Still, the counselor's assessment didn't make sense to him. It didn't jibe with what his friends and family had told him about being somebody important one day. John had been in class alongside basketball and baseball players whose grades were worse than his. They got help from tutors, and some had received full scholarships to college. How could his grades not be good enough when he was doing as well as or better than other athletes?

John decided to have a long talk with Coach Dahner about his desire to go to college and play baseball. Surprisingly, the coach wrote a letter on his behalf to Southern Illinois University in Carbondale (SIUC). The letter outlined John's educational background and highlighted his talents on the baseball field. As a result of the letter, SIUC agreed to let John enroll as an unclassified student for one quarter. If he completed his courses that quarter with a designated grade point average, school officials said, he could enroll as a matriculated student the following quarter. If all went according to plan, John could pursue a scholarship after he became fully matriculated. He planned to enroll in SIUC in January, 1961. It meant he could earn money before he enrolled. He decided to spend that time living and working with his father and brother, Charles, in Indianapolis. The next two seasons would teach him about the importance of focus and unwavering deter-mination.

Mose Lambert believed men should work with their hands. Though he accepted Charles' enrollment in college and John's plans to attend after that summer, his sons were to follow his rules while they were living under his roof. That meant they would work with their hands as laborers, and they would work hard as laborers to earn their keep.

Each morning, Mose took his two sons to Union Hall in downtown Indianapolis where they and dozens of other black men would sign in to work at a job-site for the white-owned Baker, McHenry & Welch construction company. After everyone signed in, the job-site manager would arrive and call out the names of eight or nine of the men who'd signed in—depending on how many the job required—to work that day. Once selected, workers went from site to site digging ditches or moving debris.

During that first week, John's father and brother were called every day, but his name never was. Frustrated, he decided to take matters into his own hands. Right after

Mose and Charles left for a site, John went into the office to talk to the receptionist.

"Every day I come in here and sign my name, and every day nobody calls me," John said. "What do I have to do to get sent out on a job?"

"You'll just have to wait your turn," the receptionist replied, quickly returning to her work.

Undeterred, John asked to speak with the manager's son about the situation. When the man came out into the lobby, John repeated his question about being sent out on a job.

"Tell me this," the man responded, "why should we send you out on a job ahead of these other men?"

"Because I'm a student and I'm trying to make money so I can go to college next year," a confident John responded.

"There are men here with families and kids and they need jobs for their livelihood. You don't." With that, the man turned and walked away.

John sighed heavily and went home. He'd done all he could. All that was left was to come back the next morning and sign in all over again. But something he said must have gotten through to the manager's son. He received a call at home to go out on a job that very day. From then on, John was employed for the rest of the summer and fall as weather permitted.

How strange it is, John thought, the way people say one thing and do another. Speaking up for himself had paid off. He had been polite, of course, but persistent. Such lessons as this one would pay John dividends more than once in the years to come. Sure, all he had accomplished by this time was the right to dig ditches. But he felt in his heart that eventually his day would come.

That summer and fall, John worked hard during the day, and he slept hard at night. It was a difficult time. He didn't know the city and he didn't know the people, so his weekends were usually lonely. But he endured the loneliness because he knew he'd be going to college soon. No doubt he'd be playing baseball on a scholarship soon after that.

CHAPTER 4

Big Man On Campus

Blacks in the country were making history participating in the Civil Rights movement by 1961. Testing desegregation practices in the South, Freedom Riders encountered overwhelming violence that year, which eventually led to federal intervention. Also in 1961, Whitney Young was appointed executive director of the National Urban League. He garnered a reputation for bridging the gap between white political and business leaders and poor blacks.[8]

It was against this backdrop that John would be entering SIU in Carbondale, Illinois. The city of 22,000 had developed simultaneously as an education center, a mercantile center and a transportation center. As the university continued to grow, the Illinois Central Railroad thrived, and the population and commerce of Carbondale grew as well. Southern Illinois University was the main supporting employer of the city, having hired nearly 40 percent of Carbondale's total labor force.[9]

John was entering SIUC harboring the hope of a full scholarship to play baseball. But that wasn't the only thing weighing on his mind. He was the first child in his family to stay on campus while attending college. There was a lot riding on his college career. Other students pondered majors, but for a Lambert child, the question was much bigger than that. Could he hold his own, both academically and economically? After all, John wasn't too far removed from his average grades and stint in a remedial reading course at East Side. The words of his high school counselor played on the edges of his mind. Maybe he *didn't* have good enough grades to make it in college . . .

His brother, Freddie Lee, traveled with him by bus to Carbondale. As the bus bumped along during the 96-mile trip, the littered lights of East St. Louis faded into the distance. John daydreamed about becoming a star baseball player for the SIUC Salukis. When the bus pulled into the station in Carbondale, John fished the conditional acceptance letter he'd gotten from SIUC out of his bag. No one was there to meet them. Maybe the coach forgot he was coming, John thought. At Freddie Lee's suggestion, he called the baseball coach, Abraham "Abe" Martin, from a payphone. John finally tracked him down at a dinner meeting. Coach Martin hadn't known John was due in that night, so he left the dinner and drove to the station to meet the young men.

Coach Martin shook hands with John and Freddie Lee and helped them load their luggage into his trunk. John showed the coach his letter and explained to him that he was enrolled in two courses for the quarter. He also told Coach Martin that he wanted to play baseball on scholarship the following quarter. The coach was honest with John, and said he shouldn't get his hopes up. In the springtime, white players on SIUC's baseball team went down South for spring training. Black ballplayers couldn't participate in training because no sponsor families would house them in the segregated South. By the time the team returned to Carbondale, Coach Martin explained, the team members would be fully conditioned and John would have to play catch-up. John nodded in understanding—but not in agreement. Coach Martin, he decided, would be proven wrong.

Coach Martin found a place for John and Freddie Lee to spend the weekend. It was with a local resident who rented rooms to college students. As he dropped them off at the man's home, the coach offered John a job in the athlete's locker room, where other athletes worked, organizing and storing the equipment. John agreed, excited about reporting for work the following weekend. When Freddie Lee left heading back home on Sunday, he was proud of John but sad to leave him alone at the sprawling university.

John became acclimated quickly, living in a rented room at a black couple's home, the Edgars. He shared a dorm-sized room with another student, Joe Williams, from Cairo, Illinois. Crowded as it was, their room still had more space than John's did back home. He and Joe became fast friends, though Joe never understood John's fierce love of baseball. He teased John mercilessly for once spending $25 on a baseball glove.

Life at the Edgar's was enjoyable. It was located on

Green Street, one mile from SIUC's campus, right next door to William and Eurma Hayes. The Hayes family reminded John of his own. Well-known and well-liked in the town's black community, most of the Hayes' 10 children were active at Bethel African Methodist Episcopal (A.M.E.) church. John met the Hayes family through a young college student named Joyce Harris who visited their home regularly. Joyce visited the Hayes family because her fiancé, Richard Hayes, was away in the military. She stayed in touch with the family to keep in touch with him. William and Eurma treated her as a member of the family.

John became friends with Joyce and saw her on campus often. They both worked at SIUC's dining hall, Thompson Point Cafeteria. Like John and Richard, Joyce came from a large family. She was third-youngest in a family of 12 and was originally from a small town in Illinois just north of Cairo, called America. A regular churchgoer, Joyce attended Bethel A.M.E and was a member of the choir.

Every guy on campus knew that Bethel's choir had the cutest girls. John and his friends stopped by the church after choir rehearsal many a Saturday, hoping to catch the eye of some coed. When Joyce told John that her younger sister, Martha Ann, would be attending SIUC the next fall, he knew he had to meet her. When he did, John was immediately smitten. Martha Ann joined the choir at Bethel, too, so John stepped up his visits to Saturday choir rehearsals. He didn't want to miss a chance to walk Martha Ann home.

John spent weekdays in class and most weekends working in the locker room or the campus cafeteria. He hadn't lost site of his dream to play baseball, though. He expected to segue easily into playing once the team returned from spring training. But when they got back, unfortunately for John, things happened just the way Coach Martin had said they would. At practice, John's timing was off and he was nowhere near the level of fitness his teammates were. He ended up playing with the sophomore team for one season, delivering a below-average performance on the field. He would never regain the ground he'd lost during that crucial first quarter. He stopped playing baseball after that season.

John decided to stick it out at school, surprising himself by earning Bs in his first two classes. A flicker of determination returned, and he made the decision to succeed in college. When he arrived at SIUC, he was wary and filled with uncertainty. Now he'd been tested. He knew what it was going to take, and he also knew that he had what it took. But he had to find a way to earn money for tuition. He held several different jobs at SIUC by this time, including a janitorial position and one in campus security. Still, he was struggling to make ends meet. When he took Martha Ann out for dinner, he didn't order food for himself. He'd tell Martha Ann he wasn't hungry. The truth was that he couldn't afford two meals.

John was barely scraping up enough money for school, books, and his rented room. One day as he was walking through campus, he saw a familiar face from back home. Roosevelt Johnson, who'd been a star quarterback at East Side's old rival Lincoln High, called out his name. The two exchanged greetings and Roosevelt began to talk about what he liked about SIUC. Roosevelt said he was a member of Kappa Alpha Psi fraternity. At the time, John didn't even know what a fraternity was.

"Man, you should come by the frat house," Roosevelt said, regaling John with stories of how a frat brother would give him the shirt off his back, and how being in a fraternity meant he would always have instant, lifelong friends. Sufficiently enticed—John was still insecure about his place in a world where classmates got spending money by mail and he lived paycheck to paycheck—John decided he wanted to try to pledge the following quarter. If he became a Kappa, he could live in the Kappa House and get three meals a day included with his rent.

Kappa Alpha Psi accepted John, and he ended up pledging for two quarters. To participate in pledging activities, he had to maintain a C average. It wasn't easy. Between juggling classes and staying away from Kappa big brothers, it was a busy, stressful time. He called Freddie Lee back home some evenings, and his brother was happy to lend a sympathetic ear. Like John, Freddie Lee wasn't familiar with fraternities and he didn't understand their rites of passage. It sometimes saddened his brother to hear what John was going through.

The final week of pledging, commonly known as "Hell Week," was the worst for John and the other pledges. They were all required to carry around three bricks apiece wherever they went, besides wearing sunglasses. They were kept up late every night and had to report to the Kappa House regularly, where they were drilled on fraternity history. Thank goodness for the dean of pledges, who acted as a go-between for pledges and their big brothers. When John finally became a Kappa and got a paddle emblazoned with the year 1963, he did so as his frat brothers' equal. He'd even scraped up enough money to buy a Kappa ring. By then, there was no doubt in his mind that he finally belonged. He would live in the Kappa House part of his sophomore year and all of his junior year.

The fraternity helped John immensely. To him, becoming a Kappa meant he was joining the black middle class. It also helped him establish ties with young men from other backgrounds. Through Kappa Alpha Psi, John met and developed lasting friendships with many young men, including a student from Milwaukee, Booker Thomas and a student from Detroit, Arkles Brooks. Fraternity life also boosted John's self esteem. Being on the same level with guys from these and other cities helped dissipate the cloud of discontent that had been with him since his father had left home years before. Fraternity life may not be for everyone, but for John it was just right. Here was a group of peers who cared about each other, and the experience helped John carve out a clearer sense of himself, of his world, and maybe even of his destiny.

John's chest swelled with pride when he bumped into Coach Abe Martin on campus one day that year. The coach was surprised to see that John was still enrolled. The baseball scholarship hadn't panned out, but John was well on his way to earning a Bachelor's Degree in Sociology.

CHAPTER 5

Country Girl, City Boy

By the time John became a Kappa in 1963, he and the cute country girl who had come to college in 1961 were going steady...despite the ups and downs that accompanied their relationship at first. Without a doubt, Martha Ann Harris was everything that John had prayed for. She was from the country, she was beautiful, and she was sincere. John had a lot of respect for her, and he hoped he could marry her someday.

He'd been walking her home ever since Joyce introduced them. It became a weekly thing—him stopping by the church after choir rehearsal and walking her to the room she rented at a home on Oak Street. Whether it was Martha Ann wondering if he'd come by on a particular Saturday, or on the same day getting testy when he greeted her with "Hey, momma" in the vernacular of the time—"I'm not your momma," Martha Ann snapped back—they definitely liked each other. A lot. John made sure he was around as often as possible, whether Martha Ann was going home or heading off to class. It hadn't been easy pledging and being a boyfriend at the same time. There were certain days when John couldn't be seen talking to a girl. And during Hell Week, he hadn't been able to go out socially at all. But he and Martha Ann stayed in regular touch with each other, and had gone to the annual Kappa Dance together.

When school ended for the summer in 1963, Martha Ann went to stay with one of her sisters, Ruth, and her husband, Dr. James Hedrick, in Gary, Indiana. By this time, John and Martha Ann were becoming more serious. John knew Martha Ann loved him, and he knew he adored her. They wrote each other regularly, and John loved getting letters from Martha Ann. John missed her so much that he couldn't wait until fall to see her. One day out of the blue, he told her he was coming to Gary for a visit. She dismissed it and expected not to see him until school resumed. When the doorbell rang the following Friday afternoon and John was at the door, Martha Ann couldn't believe her eyes. It took a few moments to register with her.

"I told you I was coming to see you," John said, smiling at her surprise. "Aren't you going to let me in?"

When she finally did, she excitedly introduced him to her sister and brother-in-law. They welcomed John like family. They didn't have room for him to stay there, so they called another sister in Gary, June Morgan. She said she and her husband, Wilbur, were happy to have John stay the weekend. Martha Ann rode with them to take John to their house. As Ruth and James had done, June and Wilbur welcomed John like family. The next morning, June made a country breakfast of sausage, bacon, eggs, pork chops, cabbage, toast and orange juice. It was wonderful, and it was a defining moment for John. He wanted to be a part of this family and he knew then that it was just a matter of time before he and Martha Ann would marry.

As they grew closer to each other, John and Martha Ann went through the rounds of introducing each other to their respective brothers and sisters. Nearly all of John's 10 brothers and sisters and Martha Ann's 11 brothers and sisters met each other. Sisters and brothers were easy, though. The true test would be how John's mother felt about Martha Ann and how Martha Ann's father felt about John. When John introduced Martha Ann to his mother, things went well. He could tell by the way his mother smiled and spoke to Martha Ann that she really liked her. He was happy and relieved at the same time. He and Martha Ann had decided to get married the following year. John's mother was surprised at first. Why would they get married when he had one year left in college? Once she met Martha Ann, though, her doubts vanished. She could tell John was happy. She gave them her blessing. John would meet Martha Ann's father, Samuel "Daddy Harris" Harris, and her stepmother, Daisy "Miss Daisy" Harris that same year. (Martha Ann's birth mother Ida Belle Buren Harris had died when she was just a toddler.)

The year that John met Daddy Harris and Miss Daisy, 1964, Lyndon B. Johnson signed the Civil Rights Act into law, giving federal law enforcement agencies the power to prevent racial discrimination in employment, voting, and the use of public facilities. It was also the year that Rev. Martin Luther King, Jr., was awarded the Nobel Peace Prize. Jazz saxophonist John Coltrane recorded "A Love Supreme," in 1964.[10] On this particular day in 1964, John L Lambert was considering what he would say to *his* love supreme's father.

Martha Ann had told him plenty about her father. Daddy Harris was the Sunday School superintendent at St. Paul A.M.E. Church in Mounds, Illinois, so John and Martha Ann would be required to accompany him to Sunday School and church that Sunday. She'd also told him her father rode a horse-and-buggy and sold fruits and vegetables in town. But John didn't know just how far outside town the Harris family lived until that first visit.

He and Martha Ann were driving along the unlit road near her home when Martha Ann said matter-of-factly, "You better slow down or you're going to hit my daddy." Startled, John reduced speed and coasted for the next few yards to the farm house's driveway. He hadn't seen his future father-in-law riding a horse-and-buggy along the side of the rode. John wondered to himself: Just how country is this girl?

By the end of the weekend, John was impressed and inspired by Martha Ann's father. John had sized him up as a sincere man who loved his daughter very much. She was the baby of the family, after all. John saw Daddy Harris as a man with no real agenda other than to be kind. His father-in-law to be talked often about how important it was to love others and to obey God, who he fondly referred to as "the Big Boss." What John enjoyed most about this visit was watching Daddy Harris lead a Sunday School class of two or three people. It left a deep impression on John, seeing this dedicated man fulfilling his commitment to God in his small church.

On April 18, 1964, the night before John and Martha Ann's wedding at Bethel A.M.E. in Carbondale, Daddy Harris took John aside for a final word of advice. Fortunately for John, he'd been warned by husbands of the other Harris girls about "the talk." Good thing. He wouldn't have known how to react otherwise.

"Now son, there may be some times when you may get angry or upset at Martha Ann," Daddy Harris said. "But if you ever get so upset that you feel like you have to raise a hand to her, why, you can just send her on back home. Because she's still my daughter, and she always has a home here." How dear this farmer was! He wanted to protect his daughters and he didn't want any harm to come to them. There must be a lot of love in this family, John thought to himself.

* * *

The weather was clear and cool the afternoon of April 19, 1964. Bethel's sanctuary and basement were adorned in burgundy and white for the wedding and reception. Martha Ann wore a long white wedding gown that she'd borrowed from her sister, June, and long white gloves that Mrs. Eurma Hayes had made. Martha Ann's sister Joyce, who'd been married for three years by this time, was the matron of honor. John's Kappa brother, Jesse Reed, was his best man. Kappa Booker Thomas sang "The Twelfth of Never" and the "Hawaiian Wedding Song" for the occasion, and one of Martha Ann's nieces, Yolanda Taylor, was the flower girl. After the wedding reception at Bethel, the happy couple drove to the Kappa House for a second reception. They were eager to begin their new life together.

John and Martha Ann decided to stay in Carbondale after they got married. They lived in a rented apartment on Walnut Street. John decided to look for work back in his hometown, East St. Louis, because he heard he could make more than $1.25 an hour there. He spent a week in the city, pounding the pavement. He caught the bus back and forth, throughout and around town, filling out applications at hotels and corporate offices. Unfortunately, no one was hiring. John was ready to count his losses and head back to Carbondale when he ran into his former coach from the sandlot baseball team, James H. Davidson. They hadn't seen each other in a long time. After the two shook hands, Mr. Davidson asked him what he was doing back in town.

"I'm looking for work," John said, explaining how he hadn't found anything all week.

"Look here, son," Mr. Davidson said. "If you go to the railroad station tomorrow morning, I guarantee they will hire you. You'll make good money there, too."

John didn't wait until the next morning. He went to the railroad station right after he said goodbye to Mr. Davidson. Mr. Davidson had been right. John got a job on the spot, earning $2.65 an hour. He worked there all summer long and went back and forth to Carbondale on the weekends. The money he earned at the railroad station was enough to cover his and Martha Ann's apartment and part of his tuition the following year. Good thing. By then, Martha Ann was expecting their first child—a boy—so she and John needed all the extra

money they could get. They named their new baby boy
Avery Jon.

1965 was a whirlwind year for the young family. Avery
was just a few months old. He had been born healthy
despite doctors' dire predictions of mental or physical
defects because Martha Ann had contracted rubella while
she was pregnant. Martha Ann dropped out of college
to take care of Avery with plans to return later. John
decided to enroll in the quarter-long Practice Teaching
program that was required for students pursuing a
teaching license. He wanted to get a teaching license
just in case he couldn't find work elsewhere once he
graduated.

He applied and was accepted to do his Practice
Teaching at his alma mater, East Side, under the direction of a full-time classroom teacher. Practice Teaching
didn't pay, so John had to find another job to support
his growing family which had moved to East St. Louis
by this time. He decided to get work driving cattle in
the stockyards in the afternoons. After teaching in the
morning, John went home and changed into ragged, worn
clothes and a hat that he pulled way down over his eyes.
He rode the State Street bus from his apartment to the
stockyards. As the bus bumped along the road to its
final stop, John saw some of his students getting on
the bus after their classes were ending for the day. They
probably didn't recognize John in his raggedy getup,
but he definitely recognized them.

Once at the stockyard, John drove hogs from one pen
to another. Farm trucks let out 30 or 40 hogs in the
yard, and John led groups of the animals into various
pens. After he got one group of hogs inside a pen, he'd

lock it behind him, open up another gate, and continue on with the next group until they were all contained. Herding the big animals meant trekking through a maze of foul-smelling waste, slop and mud. He looked forward to the day when he could get a professional job.

In the meantime, John needed a source of income. He took a job at Guccione's Supermarket in East St. Louis. He knew he wouldn't be at the supermarket long, but he needed to make some money while he pursued work in another field. It would turn out to be an unforgettable experience.

John worked at Guccione's during a particularly heated period in the Civil Rights Movement. The Voting Rights Act had just passed following the Selma-to-Montgomery March, which garnered the nation's attention when marchers were beaten mercilessly by state troopers at the Edmund Pettus Bridge. It was the same time period when the Watts area of Los Angeles exploded into violence following the arrest of a young male motorist charged with reckless driving. At the riot's end, 34 were dead 1,032 were injured and 3,952 were arrested.[11]

Guccione's was not immune to racial prejudice. The family-owned market was known for hiring blacks to stock shelves instead of as higher-paying cashiers. True to form, John had been hired as a stock-boy. One black organization, the 25-year-old interracial Congress of Racial Equality (CORE) known for its direct-action tactics,[12] set its sites on the supermarket. Its members picketed along the sidewalk in front of Guccione's regularly. They sometimes came into the store, filled shopping carts with groceries, rolled the carts up to a cashier, had their groceries rung up—then pretended that they'd forgotten their money. Frustrated store employees had to restock full baskets of food. The store manager tried to deter CORE tactics by demanding that black shoppers prove they had payment *before* their groceries were rung up, so CORE members adjusted their tactics. They began filling carts with groceries, leaving them near cash registers and simply walking out the front door.

It was a tense environment to work in. John often had to walk through picketers as he came in to work. On one such day the store manager asked John to take a ride in his car with him. John obliged. The two drove for nearly 45 minutes, all the way into St. Louis, mostly in silence. The store manager pulled into an alleyway and put the car in park. John was uneasy. His boss turned to face him and said he was very troubled by the picketing at Guccione's. He also said he didn't know what to do to end it. After a time, he put his car in gear and drove back to the market. Was he wanting John to possibly intervene on his behalf? Was he indirectly seeking his advice? Was he seeking a sympathetic ear? He never mentioned anything to John again about the drive or their conversation. John didn't know how to take the unsettling incident.

The mid-to-late 60s were difficult years in America. A lot of people were unhappy and a lot of them were angry. John was just looking forward to working someplace else.

John had been traveling north to Springfield, Illinois, in search of a state government job when he wasn't working at Guccione's. He thought he could get into government work with his degree and job experience. It took several interviews at several offices, but John was finally offered a job as a Disability Claims Adjudicator for the Federal Disability Program, an arm of the Department of Rehabilitation Services. His work would include making eligibility determinations on applications filed under the Social Security Disability Program. He accepted the job. As soon as he did, he ran to a pay phone in Springfield and called Martha Ann in East St. Louis. The two were ecstatic. He was going to be making $410 a month! John and his family moved to the capital city of Springfield, Illinois, on May 15, 1965.

Springfield is located at the intersection of Interstates 55 and 72 with Chicago 200 miles northeast, St. Louis 100 miles southwest and Indianapolis 195 miles due east. It became the capital in 1837 with the assistance of young Abraham Lincoln, who lived in Springfield until he left to become the sixteenth president of the United States in 1861. Springfield was home to insurance companies, health care companies, medical training and research, and scores of state, regional, and national associations.[13]

John and Martha Ann found a place to live in Springfield only after nail-biting anxiety. A friend had told them repeatedly by phone that he'd have a place for them whenever they moved to the city, but he was surprised when the young couple took him up on his offer and showed up unannounced. At first he offered to let them rent a room at his landlord's house, but John and Martha Ann insisted that he locate a private place for them. He finally did, and the family settled into a rental home on Eighteenth Street (later named Martin Luther King Drive).

Martha Ann began looking for a church to attend right away. She'd grown up A.M.E., so she checked the telephone book for A.M.E. churches first. She was excited to find two of them, St. John and St. Paul. She called St. Paul first—the name struck a nostalgic chord with her since it was the name of the church she grew up in—but no one answered the phone. She hung up and called St. John. The first lady of the church, Mrs. Juanita Stewart, answered. She was open and friendly with Martha Ann, telling her about the worship service and where the church was located. When Martha Ann got off the phone, she knew she wanted to go to St. John.

She told John about it, and he was happy for her. He knew she was accustomed to attending church, and that she was born-and-bred A.M.E. John, on the other hand, was only attending church sporadically. The majority of his church attendance after entering college had been to see Martha Ann after choir rehearsal at Bethel. When Martha Ann joined St. John, she did so alone with baby Avery. She joined the sanctuary choir right away.

Martha Ann often talked to John about the church and how friendly and warm all its members were. After some time passed, John began thinking about his hometown church, St. Mark Baptist. God had opened many doors for him since then. He thought he should at least consider going back to church. After mulling it over for awhile, John decided he wanted to go back to church—but he wanted to go back to the Baptist church in particular. He braced himself to tell Martha Ann. He knew she wouldn't like the idea of them going to separate churches, but that's the way things were going to be.

"I decided I want to go back to the Baptist church," he told her one afternoon, steeling himself for her reply.

"Okay," she responded. "You go ahead and look around at the Baptist churches here. Once you find one that you like, then we can all go together as a family."

John was stunned. Her reaction was the opposite of what he'd expected. He'd been prepared to respond to a major disagreement—but not to a conciliatory statement like the one Martha Ann had just made. The ball was back in his court. He visited two local Baptist churches, Pleasant Grove and Union. For several months he attended one or the other off and on, going once every two-to-three weeks. He wasn't quite ready to make a full-time commitment, though. He remembered what his wife had said about the family attending church together. He knew he wasn't being fair to her wishes. Why did he want to take Martha Ann out of the church she grew up in, John asked himself, the church they'd gotten married in, to put her in a setting where *he* wasn't even fully committed? He began reflecting on how he'd found his wife in the A.M.E. Church. He even did some research on the church's historical background. He was impressed with what he found.

The denomination's story actually began with a young man who would eventually become its first bishop, Richard Allen. Born into slavery in 1760 and converted to Methodism at the age of 17, Richard knew almost immediately he was called to preach. His owner allowed Richard and his brother to join a Methodist class meeting, led by a Delaware farmer. Their owner was so taken by Richard's sincerity that he allowed interracial religious gatherings on his property. Finally, converted to Methodism himself, Richard's owner arranged for the Allen brothers to buy their freedom.

Rev. Richard Allen began his career as a preacher of the gospel part-time. He worked as a teamster hauling supplies for General George Washington's army, preaching along his route. After the Revolution, Rev. Allen became a popular preacher in the Mid-Atlantic States. In 1784, when the Methodist Episcopal Church was formed in Baltimore, Rev. Allen was one of only two black preachers present. He was licensed as a preacher in St. George's Methodist Episcopal Church in Philadelphia and began preaching in the new church. Preaching at separate services to the black members of St. George, Rev. Allen brought in more black members than the church could hold. By 1787, experiencing abuse and discrimination at the hands of the white members, Rev. Allen led his flock out. In 1794, they organized their own congregation. Rev. Allen was ordained by the Bishop as the Methodist Episcopal Church's first black deacon. His joy would soon be overcast when the Methodist Episcopal church claimed ownership of the church property. Rev. Allen launched a legal battle that he eventually won in 1816.

After the victory, he issued an invitation to other black Methodist Episcopal congregations to assemble in convention. There were 16 representatives at the convention in Philadelphia, representing churches in Delaware, Pennsylvania, New Jersey and Maryland, which joined together to form the African Methodist Episcopal Church in April, 1816. They elected Rev. Allen as their first bishop. The group determined to adhere to traditional Methodism and adopted a doctrine and discipline almost identical to that of the Methodist Episcopal church.[14]

Today, there are nearly three million A.M.E. church members around the globe in Africa, the West Indies, South America, Europe, Canada, The Bahamas, Bermuda and throughout the continental United States.[15] The mission of the A.M.E. Church is to minister to the spiritual, intellectual, physical and emotional needs of all people by spreading Christ's liberating gospel through word and deed.[16]

The A.M.E. Church history touched John's sensibility regarding the need for racial justice. It was exactly where he needed to be. He added his name to the roll at St. John A.M.E. Church.

The next two years were busy ones for John and Martha Ann. Martha Ann got a job at Bell Telephone and she and John began saving money so she could go back to school. Thanks in part to the friends they met at church and work, they had a busy social life. They dined out and visited with family and friends regularly. By this time, there was plenty of family to visit. John's brothers, Jerry and Freddie Lee, had recently moved to Springfield with their wives and children. And James and Georgetta Slaughter, almost family because Martha Ann's brother-in-law, Richard Hayes, was Georgetta's brother, lived in Springfield. The Slaughters were an important connection for the Lamberts. They owned and operated Kiddie Kollege, a daycare in Springfield that many black children—including Avery—attended. Theirs was the first black-owned daycare in the city.

John joined a softball league while Martha Ann joined a volleyball team. They were family affairs, so they took turns taking Avery with them. Most of their socializing occurred around food, whether it was picnicking or barbecuing. Both John and Martha Ann loved to be around people, and John had a knack for planning events for big groups. Busy schedules notwithstanding, family life was their focal point. By the spring of 1967, they were expecting their second child. Bryon Keith was born on November 11, 1967.

Despite a tournament game in John's softball league that kept him away on an occasional Sunday, he and Martha Ann attended church regularly. Sunday School, however, was a different story. John was bored there. He and Martha Ann were two of a handful of twenty-something-year-olds who attended Sunday School. Besides classes for young children, St. John had only one adult Sunday School class with a few older members attending. It seemed as if people left Sunday School after they graduated from high school and didn't return until they were grandparents. With his sights set on eventually becoming Sunday School superintendent—he admired his father-in-law's dedication and commitment in that role—John approached the new pastor, Rev. Gregory G.M. Ingram, with a proposition: Could he develop a Sunday School class for the younger adults of the congregation? Rev. Ingram agreed, and the *19-38 Class*—so named for the age range of its members—was born.

John thought the 19-38 class would be his legacy. He fully expected it to lead into his becoming superintendent of the Sunday School, after the current superintendent, Peggie Senor, left. But she didn't leave. The closest John would ever get to becoming superintendent was the assistant position. His aspirations didn't dampen his enthusiasm for the 19-38 class, though. He was determined to make the new class a lively, entertaining one, filled with real-world examples that young adults could relate to. He added family-focused stories to each week's class, sometimes touching on current affairs. He'd prayed for at least two students to attend, but God had bigger plans. The 19-38 class eventually drew 28 regulars, with members participating in colorful discussions that added depth and meaning to age-old Bible stories.

John was pleased. With God's help, he'd started an adult class from scratch, and drew record numbers to Sunday School. People accustomed to dropping off their kids for church were now regular Sunday School attendees. Impressed with his commitment, Rev. Ingram appointed John a steward, an A.M.E. Church officer whose duties include taking care of church finances, handling the pastor's salary, and caring for the pastor's welfare.[17] The position appealed to John's ambitious, people-loving spirit. Still, something was missing from his spiritual life. He hadn't yet returned to the full relationship he'd had with God as a young boy. Time would tell if he ever could.

John L age 8

The 1959-60 East St. Louis High School Flyers

The Flyers Baseball Team

John and Martha Ann's wedding on April 19, 1964. Pictured are John, Martha, Daddy Harris and Miss Daisy

John and Martha Ann outside Joyce and Richard's home in Carbondale in 1973

Avery, 3 mos.   **Bryon at 4 mos.**   **Cheryl Ann at 3 mos.**

58

John, Martha and children at family dinner, November 1973

John's Family. Back row: Velma, Joyce, Delores, Ida, Evelyn, Mom (Mildred Lambert). Front row: Dad (Mose Lambert), Freddie, Jerry Charles, Alvin, John, and Elmer.

Private business venture from start to finish.

60

John barbequing for picnic, September 1990

John and Rev. Sammy Hooks after John's trial sermon at St. John A.M.E. Church in Springfield, May 1983

John at Service of Ordination for Deacon

John watches construction work on the Dept. of Revenue building, Springfield, April 1981

Talking with children during run for School Board, Springfield

Lambert family during School Board meeting after John had been elected. Avery, Martha, Bryon, and Cheryl Ann wear campaign T-shirts. Other family and friends in background.

64

President Jimmy Carter speaking at Lincoln Land Community College in Springfield, Illinois, September 1980. John sits on front row.

At the Million Man March, Washington D.C., October 1995

John in meeting with Illinois Governor Jim Edgar

John with Attorney Johnny Cochran at IAMG news conference, March '99

Substance of Hope Committee after first meeting in Lambert home, November 1998. Back row: Cynthia Newman, Rev. Galda McCants, Marie Leddell, Seretta Thomas, Jerry Lambert, Valerie Lambert, Rev. Gary McCants. Front row: Jerelene Northern, Martha Lambert, Rev. John L Lambert.

Lambert Family, August 2002. Front row: Jermanie, Nicole, Jessica, Cheryl Ann. Second row: Debbie, Regina. Third row: Bryon holding Jarod, Martha, John. Back row: Avery, Sharon

**Rev. John L Lambert in front of Bethel
A.M.E. Church, Indianapolis, 2001**

CHAPTER 6

Sunny and Cloudy Saturdays

John, Martha Ann, five-year-old Avery, and two-year-old Bryon were settling into a comfortable family life by 1969 when they purchased their first home on Gregory Court in Springfield, Illinois. John wasn't many months removed from finishing up payments to the state of Illinois for his mother's ADC bill. It had almost cost him their mortgage loan even though the Responsible Relatives Act had been repealed by then. Martha Ann had worked briefly at the Office of Education and was now working at Horace Mann. John and Martha Ann had worked hard and prayed hard to get where they were. And it was finally starting to pay off.

2049 Gregory Court was a red brick house located in a mixed-race, middle-class neighborhood on the southeast side of Springfield. Two blocks east of the high school Avery and Bryon would later attend, it was filled with young families just like the Lamberts. The house had one bathroom, a backyard, and a finished basement. The basement came with its own bar. The Lambert's backyard wasn't fenced in. Neither were the three homes to their right. It made for plenty of running and playing room when family and neighborhood kids came over.

The neighborhood was so friendly that the next-door neighbor's cat, Tiny, became a fixture on the outer ledge of the Lambert's living room window. It made perfect sense when the neighbors, Jim and Linda South, gave the cat to them. After all, Tiny spent more time with the Lamberts than the Souths.

It was the kind of neighborhood where kids caught fireflies in the summertime and had to be home before their porch-lights were on. It was exactly the kind of place where John and Martha Ann wanted to raise their family.

In October, 1969, John left the Federal Disability Program—only after long consideration and much coaxing—for another government job at the newly created Bureau of the Budget. Illinois' Governor, Richard Ogilve, had created the bureau to track and regulate the budgets of state government agencies. But he wanted more than accountants working with these agencies. He wanted people with experience analyzing programs to track how the money in each agency was being spent. In addition, Governor Ogilve wanted to hire blacks in high-ranking, visible roles within the Illinois state government.

Blacks had helped the republican governor get elected, and he hadn't forgotten it. He appointed blacks as directors of the Illinois Bureau of Investigation, (the state counterpart to the FBI), the Department of Children and Family Services, and the Department of Registration and Education. In addition, he hired a black man to lead the Model Employer Program and a black woman to manage the Fair Employment Practices Commission. The governor worked hard to demonstrate inclusiveness, and he surrounded himself with people who did the same.

The Bureau of the Budget's executive recruiter, Ivy Leaguer John Linton, was the first to approach John about a position as a Budget Analyst at the new agency. John was reluctant. Like most other state government workers, he had Civil Service Code protection at his current job. It meant that he could only be fired *for cause*. A new administration, which changed with each election cycle, couldn't come in and fire an employee who was certified under the Civil Service Code unless that employee violated an employment regulation or failed to carry out his duties. The Illinois Legislature had adopted the provision so new governors or elected officials could bring in their supporters in top positions to set policy and manage agencies. Administrative managers who head state agencies don't get certified under the Civil Service Code, and John had been offered a position not protected by the Civil Service.

John was worried about accepting the Bureau of the Budget job. He didn't say no to John Linton right off, but he didn't give him a firm yes, either. Instead, John took a few days to discuss the matter with Martha Ann and some of his friends. One friend in particular, family doctor and confidant Edwin A. Lee, convinced him to pursue the job.

"By all means, if they're interested in hiring you in this new position at this new government agency, go," Dr. Lee told John. "This is a great opportunity for you."

Finally convinced, John called Linton back to set up an interview. John ended up being interviewed by four different department managers in the bureau. They made him an offer on the spot. He accepted, and his salary went from $800 a month to $985 a month in one fell swoop. He'd be making nearly as much money as the agency directors at the Federal Disability Program job he was leaving. As if that weren't enough, he would be able to meet with the governor on budget-related work issues.

As a Budget Analyst and later Unit Chief, John analyzed state agency budgets and supervised others who did the same. He also made recommendations for fiscal-year funding levels for the governor. Hoping to gain even more credibility in state government, John decided to go back to school for a graduate degree. He enrolled in a two-year Master's Degree program for Public Administration at Sangamon State University in Springfield (later renamed University of Illinois in Springfield).

Twenty-seven-year-old John and his 26-year-old wife worked hard...but they played harder. John loved to barbecue, so he used any excuse to cook out. He had a black, garbage-can-sized barbecue pit that had rusted through the years—more from overuse than age. He always made his own barbecue sauce in a huge pot on the stove. Gram hadn't given him her recipe, but she had let him watch her make sauce, take meticulous notes, and ask an occasional question—so his sauce was very close to Gram's. He would carry the pot of sauce back and forth to the backyard barbecue pit applying it to the meat, one slab at a time, with his special applicator: a rag tied to the handle from a wooden spoon. John remained closed mouth about how to make Gram's sauce, but he was willing to tell questioners that it included mustard. With the oven fan humming, the back screen door opening and closing, and the savory smoked meat smell wafting through the air, the neighbors knew when the Lamberts were having a cookout.

They also knew when the Lamberts were having a house-party.

John and Martha Ann sure-enough knew how to throw a Saturday night house-party. They meticulously planned every detail to make sure their guests would have a good time. Martha Ann made calls to family and friends to keep track of who'd be there. She got the food ready and made sure the entire house was spotless—even though the party would be held in the basement. John took the names of the partygoers to the liquor store with him. He wanted to make sure he had everybody's favorite drink on hand. As for everybody's favorite music, that was easy: John went to the local record store and bought all of the top 40 R&B singles.

Party guests who had kids came in the front door. That way, they could drop their kids off in the living room to play with Avery and Bryon for the night. Guests without kids just came around back. They entered and went immediately downstairs to the party. Music and laughter made the floor upstairs vibrate well into the night. No matter how late the party ended, though, John and Martha Ann managed to make it to church the next morning.

Saturday nights were social hours, but Saturday mornings and afternoons were family time. John might get up early and make homemade pancakes for Avery and Bryon. On another Saturday, John and Martha Ann might be bumping into one another in the kitchen, him preparing barbecue sauce and her making potato salad for an afternoon picnic at Lincoln Park with friends and family. They were on their way to a picnic one day in 1970 when Martha Ann began having contractions. She was about to deliver her third baby, a girl, at St. John's Hospital. Proud father that he was, John dropped by the picnic after his first daughter, Cheryl Ann, was born to pass out "It's a girl!" cigars. It was September 7, 1970.

By this time, John had begun to make a name for himself in Springfield. Besides being active in school, work and church, he was active in the community. He was a member of the Springfield Club of Frontiers International, a civic organization that hosted an annual Martin Luther King Breakfast, using proceeds to fund research for the skin disease vitiligo. John was also an active member of the Springfield Alumni Chapter of Kappa Alpha Psi—he was even the chapter's polemarch (president) one year. John was also a life member of the NAACP. He was well-known and well-liked at work and in the city, and he was beginning to understand how he really could make a difference—even if it was just as a reference on someone's job application.

In 1971, John helped his sister, Velma, get a job in Springfield. She'd lived with John and Martha Ann for awhile, but when the job came through, she got an apartment in Springfield. John, Martha Ann, the kids and Velma all went to East St. Louis one weekend to visit family. After the visit, as they were about to head back to Springfield, seven-year-old Avery asked if he could ride with his Aunt Velma. John and Martha Ann agreed. John drove the Lambert's car while Martha Ann held Cheryl Ann in her lap in the front. They buckled Bryon up in the backseat. Velma followed in her car with Avery buckled into the passenger's seat. Thirty-five minutes into the trip, John was startled by what he saw in his rear-view mirror.

"It looks like Velma's falling asleep," he said more to himself than to Martha Ann, his hands gripping the wheel. As soon as Martha Ann turned around, a car slammed into Velma. Her car careened off the road, heading for the field. Once it reached the edge of the highway, it flipped over three times in the grass. Martha Ann was hysterical. John pulled off the road and had barely stopped the car by the time Martha Ann was unbuckled and out, running in the field toward Velma's now upright car. She carried Cheryl Ann in one arm and dragged little Bryon along with her free hand. John was close behind, praying "No Lord, no Lord," and Martha Ann was screaming and crying, her vision blurred by tears. When they reached the car, Velma was unbuckled and standing just outside her open car door.

"He's okay. Avery's okay," she said, dazed and staggering. The top of her car was dented in, and Avery was still buckled inside and a bump was forming on the top of his head. Martha Ann quickly passed Cheryl Ann to Velma and put Bryon's hand in John's as she reached in and snatched Avery out of the car and pulled him into a bear hug. At some point during the confusion, a passerby called the ambulance. When it arrived, John watched as they loaded Velma and Avery onboard. Martha Ann traveled with the ambulance and John followed in their car to the hospital. They sighed in relief at the news when they got there. Velma was okay and Avery had suffered only a mild concussion. John and Martha Ann were able to take their son home, as long as they kept him awake all night. They did so, gladly. The terrible car accident reminded John of the significance of God and family. John had spoken to God so many times that day. Faith and family—how precious they were. He vowed never to take them for granted.

Not long after the car accident, John's mother was diagnosed with a terminal form of cancer. She was hospitalized at St. Mary's in East St. Louis, but her stay was not ideal. John and his brothers began questioning the care she was receiving and wondered if it had something to do with her public aid status. At the request of some family members, John's brother, Freddie Lee, tried in vain to get her moved to Barnes Medical Center in St. Louis, but he was only able to get her moved to Christian Welfare Hospital just outside the city. Freddie Lee and John discussed their concerns with her new doctor, but he said her diagnosis had been proper. John and his brothers disagreed with the doctor, but what could be done? They'd gotten their second opinion.

John was at work when his brother, Jerry, called him on April 17, 1972, and told him their mother had died. John was floored. He called Martha Ann and told her the awful news. In a state of shock, John felt incapable of handling his grief. He numbly went through the motions at home and at work, planning to attend the funeral in East St. Louis later that week. John's grief became bitter when he found out her memorial was to be held at a local funeral home instead of at church. His mother had recently started attending church again after years of absence. She hadn't joined yet, but John couldn't understand why her funeral wasn't being held there.

At the funeral home, John, his brothers, and his sisters lined up to say their final good-byes one at a time. When John reached the front of the line, he leaned over to kiss his mother in the casket. Her face felt cold. He still couldn't believe she was gone.

Afterwards, the family loaded up into several cars to take their mother's body to the cemetery. As the power window to the car John and Martha Ann were in slowly rolled up, the realization of the moment finally hit him. He broke down. He cried harder than he ever had before. Martha Ann consoled him, rubbing his back and squeezing his hand, saying it was okay to cry. John knew then that his mother was gone and that he would never see her again. He felt weak at the time, but his mother's death actually strengthened him. But he wouldn't realize that until the next time he faced a family member's death.

CHAPTER 7

Business Smarts

By 1974, the year Hank Aaron broke Babe Ruth's record by hitting homerun number 715,[18] Martha Ann was graduating from Sangamon State University with a Bachelor's Degree in Children and Family Services. As planned, she had returned to school two years prior. By this time she was working as a Claims Representative for Aetna Insurance Company. John was a year into his third government job.

He was working at the Illinois Department of Children and Family Services (DCFS) as a Deputy Director of Management Services. In this position, he supervised 400 employees who were responsible for preparing and monitoring annual budgets, processing vouchers, leasing offices, and other computer service duties. He'd helped his good friend James Slaughter get a position at DCFS as well. James worked in the benefits coordination department, which determined how much funding would be allowed for wards of the state.

No doubt, John's Master's Degree in Public Administration accounted for some of his increased responsibility and corporate savvy. So did his expanding social circle. He counted attorneys, educators, and politicians among his acquaintances and allies. John had even dabbled in politics himself, volunteering at the East Side Campaign Headquarters for Governor Richard Ogilve, who was an unsuccessful republican candidate that year. John would soon learn how business relationships could help, and sometimes hinder, him.

John had taken on a business venture with James Slaughter in 1971. The two had decided jointly to open a roller-skating rink as a recreational outlet for black children and families in Springfield. It seemed like a sound business investment. James knew a man in Markham, Illinois, who'd made good money with a roller rink. John had prayed and asked the Lord's guidance for the project.

The two began looking for a place to open the rink. They wanted it to be on or near the east side of town, where most blacks lived, but they also wanted it to draw some white patrons. As it happened, James knew a man who was selling four acres on the southeast side of town that was a site well-suited for a roller rink. John and James commissioned a feasibility study with Sangamon State University. How, they wanted to know, would a skating rink in that location fare in Springfield? The outcome was in their favor. Research showed that the venture could be successful if the rink drew 15 percent of its profit from white clientele. With its proximity to Southeast High School and location in a mixed-race neighborhood, John and James moved ahead with their plans. They expected to easily achieve their profit goals.

After that came the hard part: raising money to purchase land and to get a rink built. It hadn't been easy—especially since John had never made such a large purchase before. He and James put a proposal together. They would need $360,000 to purchase the property, build the structure, and pay for all the equipment they'd need to operate the roller rink. They started with the bank, summarizing their feasibility study and their intentions to create a recreational outlet for blacks (and whites) in the city. The bank was not persuaded and would not use their homes as collateral. Fortunately for the two men, the Small Business Association (SBA) was stepping up its loans for minority entrepreneurs. When John and James went to the association with their request, the SBA liked what it saw: potential. The SBA guaranteed the loan. The two men went back to the bank and were approved for a significant percentage of the money they needed for the roller rink.

Thirty-thousand dollars short and at risk of the entire project collapsing, John and James got creative. They sold debenture bonds (certificates or vouchers acknowledging a debt) to several acquaintances at $2,000 apiece. The people purchasing debentures from John and James were willing to take a risk with the new company, knowing they weren't guaranteed a return on their investment. They hoped to make money all the same.

John remembered a man he'd met earlier who was involved in improving race relations in Springfield. The man worked at the Horace Mann Insurance Company. John decided to contact him for help; after all, their venture might very well improve race relations in the city. After a series of telephone calls and meetings,

Horace Mann agreed to purchase several debenture bonds. Now, John and James had enough money to complete the transaction. They built Springfield Skating Stadium at 1530 Taylor Avenue.

Now one year into owning the roller rink, John and James were learning a hard lesson about how blacks and whites socialize. On the average weeknight, the roller rink was filled with white teenagers listening to and requesting white music. On the weekend, it was just the opposite. The all-black crowd of mostly teenagers included family members and friends of John and James from work, church, and the neighborhood. On an occasional Monday or Tuesday night, the building might be rented for private parties. The number of customers varied by the event— but it was always all-white or all-black.

By 1975, the year Arthur Ashe became the first black winner of a major men's singles championship when he captured the title at Wimbledon,[19] John and James were averaging 1,100 paid customers a week at the Springfield Skating Stadium. They needed 2,000 to turn a profit. They went over and over their income and expenses, distraught that they weren't making money the way they thought they would.

John's day job had begun giving him headaches, too. There were rumblings in the office about how he'd supported Governor Ogilve, the losing candidate, and had somehow managed to keep his job in the new administration, with democratic Governor Dan Walker. The rumblings might not have been so loud if John hadn't been successful at convincing a large number of blacks who normally voted democrat to switch to republican during the last election. But he had, and the winds of change were blowing against him.

In the next few weeks, meetings that John had previously attended at work no longer included his name on the roster. Memos that would ordinarily come to him abruptly ceased. John heard that the new director of DCFS who'd come in with Governor Walker wanted him out. The days ticked on. John was surprised when Al Raby, a Civil Rights activist and close friend of Governor Walker's, invited him out for lunch one day. Despite Al's ties with Governor Walker, he didn't seem to harbor any ill will towards John. In fact, Al appeared to be in his corner. John decided to trust him.

"Is it true, Al? Does the new director want to replace me?" John asked once they sat down for lunch.

"Yes, it's true," Al replied. "But don't worry about it. I'm going to help find you another job. A comparable one." Years later, John would surmise that Al had been looking for John's support for Governor Walker in the next election.

John went to work the next day, listless. It was hard to function, knowing that his days on the job were numbered. He completed his projects as best he could. Fortunately, Al proved true to his word. He began arranging job interviews for John. John interviewed at the Department of Transportation, and then at the Department of Revenue. He was ecstatic when the Revenue job came through in October, 1975. He was able to leave DCFS before his inevitable termination.

The Department of Revenue hired John as a Deputy Director for Administrative Services. The job came with the responsibility of managing 500 employees who were responsible for contractual services, computer services, printing, security guard services, voucher processing, office space planning and mail and messenger services. He was also able to take his administrative assistant from DCFS into his new job.

Despite the turnaround in John's job status, he and James couldn't turn the roller rink around. At first, they tried to lease the building. When that didn't work, they decided to sell it. To the disappointment of scores of black children and families, they closed the business near the end of 1975, only two years after opening its doors. Now they were left with a building and supplies, and they were hundreds of thousands of dollars in debt. After several weeks, they sold the building for far less than market value. Next, they sold the skates and any and all remnants of the roller rink that could generate money. In the end, though, they still owed $120,000. Because the initial loan had been made to James, his wife, Georgetta, John, and Martha Ann, they were equally responsible for paying it back.

John and James discussed bankruptcy as an option. Privately, John wondered how the failed business venture would affect his and Martha Ann's credit. He called on some of his politician-friends, but none could offer assistance. He prayed with little hope for the outcome. John and James pleaded with the SBA to forgive some of the loan as it had before with other businesses. Tense weeks and multiple meetings later, the association agreed and forgave a significant portion of the remaining balance. John and James would only be responsible for $60,000 of the loan—$30,000 apiece. The SBA agreed to charge no interest and set up a 10-year payoff plan during which monthly payments would increase until the loan was paid off. The bank also placed a lien on the Lambert's home.

God blessed John and Martha Ann in the midst of the storm. Martha Ann was hired as an adjudicator for the Department of Rehabilitation Services on August 17, 1977. She didn't know it then, but she was starting what would become a 23-year career at the government agency, filled with promotions and expanding responsibility. The impact of losing the roller rink reverberated through John's business and social relationships. It was a growing experience for the 33-year-old. He'd asked the Lord to help him as an entrepreneur, and he'd learned about how tough the business world really was. He was accustomed to attracting large groups of people to support his ventures, and he'd discovered that the cause determines the crowds. He was more aware of himself, his community and his place in life than ever before. Of course, that didn't mean he was above getting advice from his big brother Charles—whether he thought he needed it or not.

He and Charles had remained close. Charles was still living in Indianapolis and had a wife and four children now, and he and John talked on the phone and visited one another regularly. During one such visit to Springfield, Charles seemed more serious than usual. He took John aside to talk to him one-on-one. He told him to read Matthew 6:33:

> But seek ye first the kingdom of God and His righteousness; and all these things shall be added unto you.[20]

John took offense. Was Charles saying he was spending too much time seeking out "all these things?" He resented the implication, but the words sunk in. It struck John that Charles had never been very religious, but God seemed to now be a key part of his life. John would come to understand why in the coming months.

Sadly, Charles had been diagnosed with cancer. After an operation to remove the cancer, things looked hopeful for a brief time. But when the cancer returned, the prognosis wasn't good. Follow-up surgery didn't improve the situation. Charles lingered for nearly 18 months before succumbing to the disease at the age of 39. It was a devastating loss for John. Charles had been his best friend in many ways, giving him sound advice and sending money when he needed it. He was more than a brother. He'd almost been like a father to John.

John, Martha Ann and the kids went to Indianapolis for the funeral. Charles had given explicit instructions to his wife: he wanted a celebration, not a mourning, when he died. The Lambert siblings honored his request. They joined his widow and children for a dinner-party at the house.

It was a bittersweet home-going.

* * *

During the next several years, while Avery played basketball and football, Bryon played football and took up swimming, and Cheryl Ann took up swimming, piano, and dance, John and Martha Ann stepped up their activities in church and the city. John was elected to the Springfield District #186 School Board in 1980. The same year, he won the Arthur W. Ferguson Award for personal achievement and commitment from the NAACP.

The following year, he won the much sought-after Layperson of the Year award from St. John A.M.E. He and Martha Ann were elated when Avery graduated from Southeast High School with honors in 1982. As a member of the school board, John was able to hand his son his diploma. He and Martha Ann sent Avery to college at the University of Illinois in Champaign that fall.

As John's son was moving away from home, his father was moving closer to home. Mose Lambert, who'd lived and worked in Indianapolis from the time he'd gone to the city 28 years before, moved back to St. Louis in 1982. Mose had kept in touch with his children through the years—some more than others—and returning meant he could communicate with all of them. Many of his children still lived in East St. Louis and St. Louis with their spouses and children by this time. Mose settled into life in St. Louis and got work as a cab driver, and he began playing checkers as a hobby. John, Martha Ann, and the kids exchanged visits with Mose on occasion.

By the time 1983 rolled around, the year Harold Washington won the democratic nomination for mayor in Chicago,[21] John and Martha Ann had paid their roller rink loan down low enough to remove the lien from their home. They also had money in savings. With it, they purchased property to have a home built in a newly created subdivision on the east side of Springfield, Pioneer Park. It took some convincing before the bank would approve the loan. The bank thought the Lamberts were over-building for the area. The implication was obvious: a house that size would be more suited to a white neighborhood. John and Martha Ann didn't sway, and they ended up getting the loan to build.

Pioneer Park was located at a crossroads of class and

culture. The single-family homes being built in the area were part of an attempt by the city of Springfield to enhance the neighborhood and its reputation. It wouldn't be easy. Due east of the new subdivision was Comer Cox Park, a place where rough-neck men and boys loitered well into the night. Directly north was the low-income, scrappy east side of Springfield. Young boys sometimes walked the streets there in groups, cursing and fussing at neighbors who crossed their path. Prostitutes even frequented the very corner where the Lamberts were building their home.

Just west of Pioneer Park was the start of the city's business district. The local branch of the National Urban League, the Amtrak station, then the main library and Abraham Lincoln tourist sites led into downtown. Downtown, the Illinois Capitol building sprawled at the center of several government buildings including the Department of Motor Vehicles, the Department of Revenue and the Department of Rehabilitation Services. Within and among were bank branches, the main post office and several city bus stops where office workers and high school children milled on any given weekday.

The Lamberts moved into their home at 1305 East Capitol Avenue, 11 blocks east of the capitol building, in late 1983. Theirs was a ranch-style, brown brick house with four bedrooms, three baths, a basement large enough to host sizable house parties—they'd planned it that way—and a one-and-a-half acre yard. Though it was one of many new homes in the area, the Lambert's home stood out. A shiny brass cross was embedded in the brick to the right of the home's front door. It had been placed there at John's insistence.

CHAPTER 8

Accepting The Call

The story of why there was a cross on the Lambert's new home actually began months before the last brick was laid. It had come as a result of the transformation that had begun taking place in John's spiritual life. Though John and Martha Ann were both active in church—attending Sunday School, weekly worship service, and some church meetings—John had begun taking his spirituality more seriously than before.

He started attending Bible study every Wednesday, taking care to do research before and sometimes after each week's class. He also began to linger after church service, discussing the sermons with Pastor Sammy L. Hooks, who had been appointed to St. John in 1980. John was searching for a way to apply the lessons of the Bible into his daily life. How could he be a better husband? A better father? A better *Christian?*

Others had noticed a change in John, and they told

him so. They expected him to go into the ministry sooner or later, but John dismissed the idea. Besides, anytime a man became active in church, someone prophesied that he would become a preacher. Not John, he thought, no way, no how. Before he was re-appointed, Rev. Ingram had named John a lay reader, an A.M.E. church member who prays and reads scripture at the request of the pastor. It had been too close to preaching for John. Already, two former lay readers, Rev. Gary McCants and Rev. Archie Criglar, had accepted the call to the ministry. John didn't want history to repeat itself. He backed out of the lay reader position soon after Pastor Hooks' arrival.

People continued to predict that John would go into ministry. He continued to deflect their words. But it wasn't so easy when his friend Rev. McCants and his brother, Jerry, told him the same thing. "The Lord has something for you," they said to John on separate occasions. "You're going to be preaching some day." John was uneasy when Rev. McCants made the prediction, but when his brother said the same thing, he got angry. Why would his brother—the closest among them since Charles had passed—say something like that? Jerry had always wanted the best for John, so why would he wish something like this on him? Worse still, John was confused by his own reaction to Jerry's words.

John, Martha Ann, and the kids went to Carbondale one weekend to visit Martha Ann's sister Joyce, who'd introduced her and John back in college, and her husband, Richard Hayes. Like any other visit, this one was filled with lots of laughter and lots of catching up. Bryon and Cheryl Ann spent time with their cousin

Richard II, while the adults laughed and talked well into the night.

On Sunday morning, they headed off to the church where John and Martha Ann had met, Bethel A.M.E. A lay reader himself, Richard served in the pulpit for part of the service that Sunday. Right after the opening hymn, he called John up to do the invocation (prayer). Surprised but obedient, John stood up and began walking towards the front. He noticed something strange when he got there. The whole area from the pulpit to the altar was lit up.

Realizing that only he could see the brightness, John prayed to himself before he prayed aloud: "Lord, help me with this. I ask you to help me with this. Please help me with this." He did the invocation and then returned to his pew seat next to Martha Ann. He was quite shaken. He willed himself to forget the strange image, though he told Martha Ann about it on the drive home.

Not long afterwards, John was at a church conference one Saturday morning in Decatur, Illinois, as a lay delegate (a church member who represents his church at a conference). He was asked on the spur of the moment to greet conference attendees. Nervous and shaking, John walked up front to say a few words on behalf of St. John. When he was finished, Rev. Wilbert D. Coleman, the pastor at Mt. Zion A.M.E. Church in Ottumwa, Iowa, took John aside and repeated what he had been hearing for the past several weeks: "The Lord has something in store for you, son." This was the first time someone he didn't know prophesied about him. Now, John was scared.

He was sweating on the drive home from Decatur.

When he got home, he couldn't sit still. Martha Ann was running errands and the kids were at their weekend activities. He didn't want to be alone, so he went to White Oaks Mall in the hopes of being swallowed up in the crowds. He walked around the shopping center, still jittery but enjoying the people as they walked by. Their voices helped quiet the noise in his spirit.

John felt only slightly better when he left the mall and headed home, but things spiraled further once he arrived. He got a phone call from his classleader. African Methodist Episcopal Church classleaders are church members who have a set number of church members assigned to them, and they act as liaisons between them and the pastor.[22] When John's classleader called, she said it was her duty to give him a scripture to read. It was Matthew the tenth chapter, where Jesus sent his disciples out on assignment. Jesus gave the disciples explicit instructions about how to witness and whom to witness to, but he also warned them about the danger they'd encounter along the way:

> "Behold, I send you forth as sheep in the midst of wolves: be ye therefore wise as serpents, and harmless as doves." —*Matthew 10:16 KJV*[23]

John got the message loud and clear: It was about ministry and it was about him. But he still wasn't ready to receive it.

He decided to ask the Lord directly. He prayed silently that night, kneeling at his bedside as Martha Ann kneeled and prayed silently beside him. He made an agreement with the Lord: If he could sleep peacefully through the night, he would know that it was people pushing him into the ministry, and not God. John laid his head on his pillow and drifted off to sleep, fully expecting to make it through the night. It was not to be. He was jolted awake at 2:30 a.m. in a cold sweat by a flash of pain across his forehead. Deep in his conscience, he knew this was his answer. It was the Lord who had been speaking to him all along.

"Martha Ann, wake up," he said as he nudged his wife awake. "My head—it's hurting. And I know why."

"Darling, it's okay. Just take an Excedrin and go back to bed. You'll feel better," she said, groggily.

"I can't. It's not that kind of pain. I know what this means."

John quietly explained to Martha Ann the strange things that had been happening to him. He reminded her about his vision in Carbondale, then he told her about the scripture from his classleader and the many messages from church members, friends and family. He also told her about his prayer the night before. He cried as he talked. Martha Ann became convinced, too: John was being called to preach. They both got dressed to go see Pastor Hooks. They wanted him to know right away—never mind that it was 3:00 in the morning.

Pastor Hooks and his wife Mary answered the door in robes and pajamas. They invited the couple in. The four talked, cried and prayed together for a full hour. Pastor Hooks listened to John and then shared words of advice. He told John what was involved in accepting the call to ministry both spiritually and practically. John was relieved and worried at the same time. He admitted to himself that part of his struggle was the thought of having to relocate. John didn't want to have to move his wife and family around to church after church, yet he knew that A.M.E. ministers were appointed at the discretion of the Bishop.[24] He wanted his children to be educated in Springfield, where they had family and friends, and he told the Lord so. The next morning, John shared his news about going into the ministry with his children at the kitchen table. He shared the same news later that morning during church service at St. John with the congregation. He cried both times, weeping in anticipation of what lay ahead.

As with other A.M.E. ministers, John's journey began with a trial sermon in 1983 at St. John. The church was so full that the ushers had to place folding chairs down the aisles to accommodate the hundreds of members, visitors, family members and coworkers on hand. At his request, Cheryl Ann played "I Surrender All" on the piano and close-as-family-friend Sonia Echols sang. Avery came home from college for the occasion and he, Bryon, and Cheryl Ann sat up front with Martha Ann. They watched as John the family man became John the preacher man before their eyes. He preached on the subject "From Excuses to Gladness."

John had no more excuses for God, and he wouldn't accept them from anyone else.

The transformation in John was immediate and all-encompassing. He wanted to convince everyone of how sincere he was in following the Lord. In his zeal, he didn't always consider how his actions were perceived by others. He immediately stopped hosting house parties. He required that his family have Bible study every Sunday during breakfast. He wouldn't allow anyone to play cards in the house—it was too close to gambling, he said. And he insisted on having prayer at the end of any visit with family members.

John knew prayer was life-changing, so he didn't think it out of line to call the superintendent of schools, Dr. Donald Meidema, and ask if he could pray with him. Dr. Meidema agreed, and John prayed with him right there in his office. When he ran for reelection for the school board, John insisted that every piece of campaign literature bear a cross. He lost the election that term. It didn't deter him. He even prayed at work when a conflict arose—on the spot with the people who reported to him. To him, he was simply acknowledging God in all his ways.

John thought that surely his wife would understand the radical change in him, but she did not. The two began to argue as a result. To John, Martha Ann wasn't being a Christian if she didn't go to Bible study or attend a church conference or accompany him to a prayer meeting at someone's home. She thought he was being overbearing, and she told him so.

By the end of 1983 when their new home was almost finished, John had a vision. It was that the house should have a cross. Martha Ann cringed as she imagined a big wooden cross in the front yard which would surely alienate the friends and family who already thought John was taking religion to the extreme. She told John her reservations. He explained to her that he actually envisioned a small cross set within the mortar joints and embedded in the brick. She sighed her relief. But their arguments continued.

John talked to Pastor Hooks about his and Martha Ann's disagreements. His advice for John was simple:

"Be patient." John was, and so was Martha Ann, and their arguments finally subsided during the next several months. John settled into his new calling and began making arrangements to pursue a Masters of Divinity Degree.

In the summer of 1984, as *The Cosby Show* debuted on NBC,[25] John had another vision. It came to him in a dream. In it, he was working around an altar, serving Holy Communion, wine, and bread. He was in a minister's robe, clearly the pastor in the setting. He knew better than to doubt God's message, and he knew exactly what the vision meant. Eventually, he was supposed to start a church.

John discussed the vision and his interpretation with Pastor Hooks. Pastor Hooks immediately supported his plans to found a new A.M.E. church. He made arrangements to contact the Presiding Elder of the district, who's responsible for ensuring that each local church under his supervision understands and complies with the policies and programs of the A.M.E. Church.[26] He would be the one to make the recommendation to the Annual Conference, but John found out that it wouldn't be easy. By the time Pastor Hooks submitted an official request, two strong objections to John's plans had already reached the district level. One implied that he was starting a cult instead of a church. The other insisted that the city of Springfield simply had no need for a third A.M.E. church. Neither was true.

Ever the analyst, John had done careful research about the capacity of black churches in the city and the attendance at those churches. Then he cross-referenced those figures with the number of blacks in Springfield. What he found was surprising, but vindicating. Only

30 percent of blacks in the city were currently attending church. That meant that a vast population of un-churched people existed that might welcome a new church. Such a church, John surmised, would not pose a threat to any church that was already open.

With the steadfast encouragement of Pastor Hooks, John stepped out on faith with his wife by his side and opened the doors to Faith Temple A.M.E. Church in their living room in September, 1984. Its mission was to reach un-churched residents of the city with the gospel of Jesus Christ. Martha Ann typed and laid out the first bulletin, Cheryl Ann played the piano, and Georgetta Slaughter donated the church's very first offering plate.

The small living room was crowded the first few Sundays with John, Martha Ann, Bryon, Cheryl Ann, and sometimes Jerry Lambert and his wife, Valerie, in attendance. Each Sunday before service and after breakfast, Bryon set up folding chairs in the living room and dining room. Martha Ann opened the front window drapes to let the light in, but kept the sheer curtains underneath closed. She selected the hymns with Cheryl Ann before each service since the 14-year-old could play only a handful of songs. It was a labor of love for John and his family, and God was about to bless them indeed.

John was ordained a deacon in 1985, just as Faith Temple was being admitted into the Fourth Episcopal District of the A.M.E. Church. The small church immediately began looking for a place that Faith Temple could call home. He and Martha Ann talked to their associates, coworkers, friends and family about their search. After several months, they found Foursquare Gospel Church. A white congregation pastored by the

Rev. Michael Tozer on the Southeast side of Springfield, Foursquare's members were willing to share their space with Faith Temple. The building's location was perfect. It was far enough from St. John and St. Paul to not draw members away, and right in the heart of a predominantly black neighborhood filled with prospective new members. The situation was ideal for Faith Temple and Foursquare Gospel. They were both looking for new sanctuaries. Rev. Lambert knew that God placed the two churches in each other's paths.

During Foursquare Gospel's morning worship, Faith Temple held Sunday School in the fellowship hall. Once Foursquare's service ended and its parishioners left, Faith Temple members moved over into the sanctuary to begin their regular worship. The two churches shared the building for nearly two years, and Faith Temple slowly began to grow. Friends of friends, coworkers, and neighborhood residents trickled in to join the church one by one. By the time Foursquare Gospel Church left for its new sanctuary, Faith Temple had enough money to take over the mortgage to the building, which was valued at more than $340,000.

Rev. Lambert was happy about the building purchase, and pleased with its location. Big families with active, energetic children lived in the surrounding community. He couldn't help but remember what it was like growing up near St. Mark Baptist in East St. Louis...especially when he caught some of the neighborhood children playing softball on the church parking lot.

By this time, Faith Temple had more than 100 members on the roll. The church's new purchase and its growing membership weren't the only things Rev. and

Mrs. Lambert had to be proud of. In 1985, Bryon graduated from Southeast High School. Like he'd done with Avery, Rev. Lambert was granted his request to hand Bryon his high school diploma during the ceremony. Bryon left home for Illinois State University in Normal, Illinois.

College for the Lambert family had come full circle from Rev. Lambert's days back at SIUC when he was the first in his family to attend college away from home. His spiritual growth was just as dramatic. He'd gone from showing up at church functions to impress a young country girl to drawing people into church as its pastor. He could see the hand of God at work in the face of every man, woman and child who joined Faith Temple.

Rev. Lambert and Martha Ann were excited about the church and its prospects for both physical and spiritual growth. Martha Ann directed the choir and Cheryl Ann continued to play the piano. Church members were slated as stewardesses, ushers, trustees and stewards. Faith Temple was a true church, with all the officers, opportunities and obligations that came with it. The church—which had a membership of 300 by now—began a monthly outreach to nearby Eastgate Manor (later Springfield Terrace) nursing home to minister to its residents.

Even with his keen organizational and administrative skills, Rev. Lambert learned a lot as pastor of his own church. He learned how to work with people who are hurting and looking for ways to turn their lives around spiritually, economically, and emotionally. He learned that one size doesn't fit all when it comes to teaching and preaching. He learned about the difficulty of turning negative outlooks into positive ones. More than anything, though, he learned that finding out how to help people would remain a work in progress.

Who needs help? Why do you help? How do you help? His late brother Charles' mantra echoed in his mind.

CHAPTER 9

Civil Servant

In 1986, playwright August Wilson received the Pulitzer Prize for *Fences*, a play chronicling the black American experience.[27] *Fences* tells the story of Troy Maxson, a garbage collector living in an industrial city in the late 1950s. Troy excelled at baseball when he was young, but he couldn't play in the major leagues because of the ban on black athletes. Troy was well past his prime by the time Jackie Robinson broke the color barrier in 1947. The experience left him bitter. When Troy's son Cory, a gifted athlete, wants to go to college on a sports scholarship, Troy is against the idea. He's sure his son will end up disappointed as he himself was years before. Troy encourages Cory to be practical—to learn a trade so he can support himself.

Rev. Lambert's dreams of playing baseball to earn money so his family could get off welfare had long faded, but even in 1986, there were still striking similarities to his life and that of the fictitious Troy Maxson. Both were hard-working employees. By this time, Rev. Lambert had worked at the Department of Revenue for 11 years. They both understood the value of practical advice. Rev. Lambert continued to pursue a Bachelor's Degree even after not making the varsity baseball team at SIUC. And they both knew the value of making decisions based on how their families—and extended families—could be affected. Rev. Lambert considered it his mission to get blacks hired into professional, promotable positions. His focus was clear. He wanted to help as many people as possible avoid the welfare trap that his family had experienced.

Rev. Lambert knew that Illinois state government hired blacks. He had firsthand experience as an employee at four different government agencies since his arrival in Springfield 17 years prior. It didn't take long to realize that getting a job was one thing. Being treated fairly on that job was another matter altogether. He couldn't help but notice the sometimes inequitable treatment of black workers. He also couldn't ignore two questions that arose and lingered in his mind: Was the state of Illinois hiring and promoting the number of blacks in accordance with its own laws? And if so, did the blacks who were employed by the state of Illinois have a platform to voice their concerns about work-related issues? The answer was no on both counts.

Rev. Lambert knew of situations where blacks were being passed over for promotions, many times training whites who would later become their supervisors. In addition, he saw blacks being placed into positions without adequate training. He decided to step out to make a change for himself and the blacks who would come after him. The Equal Employment Opportunity law was on his side. He selected a group of 15 people to serve as the board of directors of an organization that would be a watchdog for the affairs of Illinois state government and the impact that it had on blacks. He founded the Illinois Association of Minorities in Government (IAMG), which was incorporated in the fall of 1987.

The IAMG worked as an advocate on behalf of minority employees in the state of Illinois for jobs, promotions, job retention and protection against dis-criminatory acts. Rev. Lambert was its first chairman of the board. The board included representatives from several state government agencies to ensure that the breadth of issues impacting minority workers were addressed. The association developed annual dues for members and a payroll-deduction system to fund its efforts. Membership grew many times over as IAMG efforts on behalf of minority workers gained local and sometimes national attention. Minority employees from as far south as Carbondale and as far north as Chicago became active members of the association.[28]

Still fully committed to his Christian calling, Rev. Lambert was now an ordained Itinerate Elder. It meant he had reached the highest level of ordination for an itinerant minister in the A.M.E. Church. He'd achieved the educational standard set by the Doctrine and Discipline. He'd successfully completed his ministerial institute training. And he'd been judged worthy of the ordination by the Board of Examiners of the ministerial institute.[29] Rev. Lambert's character and commitment to equality paved the way for his works inside and outside the walls of his church.

The IAMG held its first board of directors meeting on January 15, 1988, the birth month of slain Civil Rights leader, the Rev. Dr. Martin Luther King, Jr. Among the association's stated goals and objectives were the following: to be an advocate for the placement, promotion, and retention of minorities; to develop a legal defense fund; to work to ensure the implementation of Equal Employment Opportunity laws, and to work closely with government officials, legislators, and the general public concerning the equality or lack thereof in the training of minorities impacted by the government.[30] The association was well on its way to meeting those goals and more.

By the time Cheryl Ann graduated from Lanphier High School in 1988—Rev. Lambert handed her her diploma like he'd done with his other two children—the IAMG had also attracted a small but influential contingent of Hispanic government employees. The IAMG even successfully lobbied to get laws passed. One such law, Public Act 86-1411 which was passed by the Illinois General Assembly in 1990, requires State Agencies that do not meet their equal opportunity goals by Equal Employment Office categories to establish necessary training programs to prepare and promote minorities in furtherance of achieving those goals.

The association kicked off a quarterly newsletter to keep its members apprised of laws and political issues affecting them. It also began hosting an annual conference to educate government employees about business skills and networking strategies. Well-known conference keynote speakers helped raise the stature and influence of the IAMG. They included activist Yolanda King, actor Ossie B. Davis, attorney Johnny Cochran, the Rev. Jesse Jackson and television and radio personality Tavis Smiley.

Rev. Lambert was proud of the association and its accomplishments. But he was even more proud of his family. The family of five had become an empty nest on the one hand and an extended family on the other. Their youngest son, Bryon, married his college sweetheart, Debbie Lobb, on September 22,1990, at Faith Temple. He and Debbie were proud parents of baby Jessica and they were living in Bloomington, Illinois. Cheryl Ann graduated from Illinois State University in mid-1992 with plans to attend Temple University in Philadelphia for graduate school that fall. Avery had married Sharon Rand in August. He and his new wife were happy and hopeful parents of their daughter, Regina, and they lived in suburban Chicago.

By 1992, more than 1,000 government employees belonged to the Illinois Association of Minorities in Government. It was a business-savvy, politically astute group thanks to the developmental workshops the association provided. That same year, Carol Moseley-Braun became the first African-American woman elected to the U.S. Senate, representing the state of Illinois. But any hope for a color-blind America were dashed when riots broke out in Los Angeles later that year, sparked by the acquittal of four white police officers caught on videotape beating black motorist Rodney King.[31] There was still much to be done before equality would be practiced among all Americans.

It was a time of reflection for many black Americans

who'd lived through the Civil Rights movement. They held their families just a little bit tighter, thinking about from whence they came. Rev. and Mrs. Lambert did the same as they helped welcome their third grandchild, Bryon and Debbie's daughter, Jermanie, into the world.

By this time, Rev. Lambert's family contentment stood in stark contrast to the IAMG. The once powerful association was not only losing clout—it was losing members. Saddled by debt and unable to pay more than a handful of administrative salaries, IAMG was no longer able to meet all of its members' needs. Phone calls were going unanswered or unreturned, as were other requests for assistance with workplace issues. Members were dropping out at a rate of 20 per month, and Rev. Lambert and the board believed their beloved association was on the brink of collapse. Thankfully, the association was still championed by high-level government workers like Audrey McCrimon, director of the Department of Rehabilitation Services. McCrimon even presented the keynote speech at an IAMG annual conference when morale among the membership was particularly low. The association's board of directors knew they needed two things to ensure IAMG's survival: a full-time employee dedicated to serving the members, and money to pay that employee's salary.

The association received money through its members' $5 monthly dues. In order to bring in more money, the board would have to ask members for a dues increase. After lengthy, heated discussion, the board decided to ask the members for $7.50 a month. When the next association meeting rolled around, board members brought up the request for a dues increase, explaining in detail why the need existed. A staunch member and supporter who'd been helped by IAMG interrupted their explanation. "This is ridiculous. This is our organization. How much money do you need? We will help you." His passionate testimony was just the kick-start that IAMG needed. The membership voted then and there to double its monthly dues to $10, effective immediately. Now the IAMG could hire an Executive Director.

The Executive Director needed to have government knowledge, organizational skills and an ability to reach legislators. The job was a good match for Rev. Lambert's skills, so he and Martha Ann discussed whether or not he should interview for it. It wasn't an easy decision. Should he consider leaving the security of his vocation to pursue his avocation? It was an important question and he knew the answer: yes. He interviewed for the job and was extended an offer. In October 1993, Rev. Lambert resigned after 18 years with the Department of Revenue and was hired as Executive Director of the Illinois Association of Minorities in Government.

Rev. Lambert's happiness about his new position would be tempered by sorrow, however. Soon after he was hired, his father was diagnosed with emphysema. Rev. Lambert had never known his father to be sick. In fact, he'd never known his father to ever need a doctor. The onslaught of his emphysema was sudden, and Mose Lambert succumbed to the illness just two months shy of his 79th birthday.

It was a time of reflection for Rev. Lambert. He reflected on his father, his family and his children. His had been a long journey, personally and professionally, and he knew there was still much to be done. As Executive Director of the IAMG, Rev. Lambert would be responsible for working as an advocate, lobbyist and conference coordinator on behalf of minority government workers in the state of Illinois. He tapped the reserves God had given him during other times of loss and he forged ahead.

Rev. Lambert was in his element—pushing minority-related state government issues on radio call-in shows and news outlets in Chicago, Springfield, and throughout the state of Illinois. Big issues and small issues, Rev. Lambert and the IAMG was there. Whether it meant traveling to Alton, Illinois, to do a presentation about IAMG for a small group of Department of Mental Health workers, or sponsoring a fundraising luncheon for a democratic hopeful for governor in downtown Chicago, the association showed up, lobbying on behalf of minority employees.

When the Illinois Department of Employment Security (IDES) announced that it was about to lay off 300 employees, 40 percent of whom were black, the IAMG took action. High-ranking association members made calls, sent letters, and scheduled meetings with department directors. They didn't stop there when IDES representatives said layoffs would proceed as planned. Under Rev. Lambert's direction, the IAMG coordinated a demonstration on the steps of the Illinois Capitol building in Springfield to protest. Busloads of association members and supporters from Chicago came out to stand alongside IDES employees to vocalize their objections.

Thanks to Rev. Lambert, legislators, A.M.E presiding elders, A.M.E. ministers and other ministers were also in the crowd, supporting their cause. Protesters failed to convince the department to cancel layoffs, so Rev. Lambert recommended that IDES find positions in other state government agencies for the employees. Rev. Lambert, other IAMG members, the governor's chief of staff and the director of the IDES met. What happened after that was something no one could have imagined. They agreed to Rev. Lambert's proposal, but went a step further. They froze hiring in other state government agencies until they could find jobs for those laid off at IDES. In the end, all of the employees who had been slated for layoffs were offered jobs at other government agencies.

The IAMG had become just that powerful.

CHAPTER 10

God Heard His Prayer

In 1995, Rev. Lambert stood shoulder-to-shoulder with hundreds of thousands of African-American men who attended the Million Man March in Washington, D.C. They each had their own agendas. Their own struggles. Their own issues. But they came together that day in the nation's capital to demonstrate the hope that is synonymous with the African-American experience.

Rev. Lambert had proven adept at facing challenges and coming out on top. From grade school to church, to college and family life, he'd managed to stay focused on the task at hand. At Faith Temple, the task was saving souls for Christ. The church had a dynamic music ministry now thanks to Rev. and Mrs. Lambert's niece, gifted musician and singer, Kelly Coleman. In addition, Faith Temple had hosted an annual conference for the Fourth Episcopal District, a political event for the Rev. Jesse Jackson, and a fundraising program for a candidate for Bishop and former St. John minister, Rev. Gregory G.M. Ingram.

To Rev. Lambert, it felt good to support the causes he believed in, in a place where he knew people believed in him: the church. His once separate worlds of church, community and politics were coming together in valuable ways for church members and city and state residents alike. Now he felt a gentle stirring in his spirit. God was leading him to a higher calling where he could use his skills to serve others. That calling was for the office of Bishop of the African Methodist Episcopal Church.

In November 1998, the Substance of Hope Committee—a group of individuals committed to the candidacy of Rev. John L Lambert for the Holy Office of Bishop of the A.M.E. Church—was launched in Springfield, Illinois. The committee was formed under the leadership of Rev. Gary McCants to develop, enhance, and add value to the overall candidacy and to contribute to the economic structure of the same by interacting primarily with other clergy and members of the A.M.E. Church throughout the connection. (Connection is how the A.M.E. Church refers to its congregations collectively).

The mission of the Substance of Hope reads as follows:

- to lead the church in the creation of intellectual and economic wealth for the A.M.E. membership and the African-American community through involvement with the many entities of the church which impact the election of Bishops;
- to utilize its members' professional skills

and experience to foster Christian growth
and educational development in the A.M.E.
Church;

- to assist the corporate church community in
recruiting, developing, and retaining
members and its leadership,
- and to provide leadership growth and create
opportunities in church government, civic,
and social environments which impact the
church in general.[32]

Substance of Hope Committee members include
Presiding Elders, clergy and laypersons from several
districts within the A.M.E. Church. Its members began
hosting monthly meetings to track Rev. Lambert's
progress on the campaign trail. Through it all, Rev.
Lambert continued working in his local church and
community.

He was selected by Illinois Governor George Ryan to
serve as a member of his Transition Team in January,
1999. That summer, Rev. Lambert won the IAMG
Tradition of Leadership Award, which was presented to
him by State Representative Arthur Turner. Also in
1999, Illinois State Comptroller Daniel Hynes
appointed Rev. Lambert to his Local Government
Advisory Board to advise the Comptroller on issues
related to local government finances.

African Methodist Episcopal Church officials were
starting to take notice. Rev. Lambert's commitment to
Christ, his church, and the community were well-known
and well-regarded throughout the connection. Previous
Bishops had broached the subject of appointing him to

a different church more than once through the years. He and Martha Ann discussed the issue at length. God had answered John's prayer about not moving him while the kids were attending high school. But now that their jobs, their family, and their friends were rooted in Springfield, could he and Martha Ann handle leaving? Yes, they decided together, they could. They were excited about the prospect of beginning a new chapter in their lives. Their children had already done so.

Avery and Sharon bought and built a home in St. Charles, Illinois, and were both working for Sears Corporate Headquarters in Hoffman Estates, Illinois. They'd welcomed their new daughter, Nicole, into the world in 1994. Bryon and Debbie moved west to Oregon for a job Bryon got at Jefferson Public Radio. They'd also had another baby—a son named Jarod—in 1999. Cheryl Ann moved back to the Midwest, and was also working at Sears Headquarters by now. The blessings in Rev. Lambert's families lives foreshadowed the many blessings to come.

He had grown accustomed to meeting and speaking with dignitaries, officials and VIPs, but Rev. Lambert's heart skipped a nervous beat when he got a call from his Bishop, the Right Reverend Philip R. Cousin, Presiding Prelate of the Fourth Episcopal District, in October 2000. His telephone call came after fall church appointments had already been made. All the same, the Bishop was contacting Rev. Lambert to appoint him to Bethel African Methodist Episcopal Church in Indianapolis, the oldest black church in the city.

Rev. and Mrs. Lambert were overjoyed! He'd left the city 40 years earlier, a lonely 18-year-old saving money for college in the hope of pursing a baseball scholarship. He would be returning with a lovely wife of 36 years by his side and an esteemed record of service in the church and community.

Look at God.

The Lamberts would have to act quickly. Rev. Lambert was due to deliver his first sermon at Bethel the Sunday after the Bishop gave him the news. The church had been without a pastor for several weeks because its previous pastor had already been moved.

Bethel A.M.E. Church in Indianapolis was organized in 1836 in the log cabin home of barber Augustus Turner on Georgia Street. He had obtained an A.M.E. Discipline and used it as a guideline in organizing his group. The group petitioned to be annexed to the western circuit of the church after meeting for a time. The appeal was accepted by the Philadelphia Conference and Rev. Paul Quinn was sent as the first Circuit Rider, (a preacher who goes to different churches who don't have full-time pastors on different Sundays to hold worship service). After the church was admitted to the circuit, it built a small frame house of worship on Georgia Street. It wasn't until years later that it became formally known as Bethel African Methodist Episcopal Church. It moved into its current structure at 414 West Vermont Street in 1894.[33]

Rev. Lambert's son Avery, Avery's family, Cheryl Ann, and Rev. Lambert's brother Freddie Lee and his wife, Yvonne, surprised the Lamberts and attended his first service at the church. Church members welcomed the first couple and their family with open arms. That December, Bethel hosted a public welcome celebration for Rev. and Mrs. Lambert. City and state officials were on hand—along with prominent church leaders—to extend a warm welcome to the city's new residents.

Rev. and Mrs. Lambert returned to Springfield many times during their first several months at Bethel. There was the sendoff banquet IAMG held to honor their founder and first chairman. There was the girls-only going away party that Georgetta Slaughter hosted for Martha Ann. And there were many tearful good-byes to Faith Temple members whose only pastor of 16 years was leaving. The Lambert's tears of sorrow became tears of joy as they saw God manage their move from Illinois to Indiana. They sold their house on Capitol Avenue in three days flat. They found a house in Indianapolis almost as quickly after resolving with Bethel to sell its parsonage.

Seeing all the blessings flow from God, all Rev. Lambert could do was repeat a phrase he borrowed from his father-in-law, Daddy Harris, who'd died in 1979 never seeing his son-in-law go into the ministry: "I don't see how I done it myself."

> Now faith is the substance of things
> hoped for, the evidence of things not seen.
>
> — *Hebrews 11:1 (KJV)*[34]

Epilogue

"It takes a Kappa to ask an Alpha to speak at an Omega house," said the Bishop. The Right Reverend Philip R. Cousin was speaking to a crowd of more than 300 people about the irony of the moment. He was the keynote speaker at a dinner banquet in October, 2001 to officially announce Rev. John L Lambert as a candidate for Bishop in 2004.

The event was held at the Omega Center banquet hall in Indianapolis. Omega Psi Phi is the third oldest black fraternity in the country. Bishop Cousin is a member of Alpha Phi Alpha Fraternity, the oldest black fraternity in the country. And he was asked by the Rev. Lambert, a member of Kappa Alpha Psi Fraternity, to speak at the kickoff event.

As he addressed attendees, Bishop Cousin emphasized the importance of following your dreams. He said there is never shame associated with dreaming, but only in not attempting to fulfill those dreams. Rev. Lambert's dream was to be elected a Bishop at the General Conference in 2004, which Bethel Indianapolis is hosting.

"I'm a person of faith who's been able to achieve against long odds," said Rev. Lambert. "God has blessed me all the way from being a welfare recipient to being the pastor of the oldest black church in the city of Indianapolis. I want to serve others, help others, and use my talents to bless the people and bless the church."

God only knows what the dreamers will dream next— or what they will accomplish.

Notes

1 *Life Application Study Bible: King James Version*, Wheaton, Ill.: Tyndale House Publishers, Inc. 1997.

2 Illinois Department of Human Services News and Publications Brochures, Springfield, Ill.: Responsible Relatives. 2000.

3 Encyclopedia Britannica, Inc: Encyclopedia Britannica Online, Chicago: "Eras in Black History." 2002.

4 East St. Louis Action Research Project. Urbana, Ill.: "Economic and Population change of the mid-20th Century." The Illinois Bottomland Explorer, University of Illinois at Urbana-Champaign. 1999.

5 Indianapolis Convention & Visitors Association, Indianapolis: "Indy's Historical Timeline." 2002.

6 Encyclopedia Britannica, Inc: Encyclopedia Britannica Online, Chicago: "Eras in Black History." 2002.

7 Encyclopedia Britannica, Inc: Encyclopedia Britannica Online, Chicago: "Eras in Black History." 2002.

8 Encyclopedia Britannica, Inc: Encyclopedia Britannica Online, Chicago: "Eras in Black History." 2002.

9 City of Carbondale, Carbondale, Ill.: "A Short History of Carbondale." 2000.

10 Encyclopedia Britannica, Inc: Encyclopedia Britannica Online, Chicago: "Eras in Black History." 2002.

11 Encyclopedia Britannica, Inc: Encyclopedia Britannica Online, Chicago: "Eras in Black History." 2002.

12 Encyclopedia Britannica, Inc: Encyclopedia Britannica Online, Chicago: "Eras in Black History." 2002.

13 Springfield Illinois Convention & Visitors Bureau, Springfield, Ill.: "City facts & figures" 2002.

14 Conner Prairie Living History Museum, History Online, Fishers, Ind.: "Life in the 1880s: The African Methodist Episcopal, African Methodist Episcopal, Zion and the Christian Methodist Episcopal Churches in Indiana." Sheryl D. Vanderstel. 2002.

15 DuPage African Methodist Episcopal Church Bulletin, Lisle, Ill. "African Methodist Episcopal Church History." 2002.

16 AMEC Sunday School Union, Nashville, Tenn.: "The Doctrine and Discipline of the African Methodist Episcopal Church." 2000.

17 AMEC Sunday School Union, Nashville, Tenn.: "The Doctrine and Discipline of the African Methodist Episcopal Church." 2000.

18 Encyclopedia Britannica, Inc: Encyclopedia Britannica Online, Chicago: "Eras in Black History." 2002.

19 Encyclopedia Britannica, Inc: Encyclopedia Britannica Online, Chicago: "Eras in Black History." 2002.

20 *Life Application Study Bible: King James Version*, Wheaton, Ill.: Tyndale House Publishers, Inc. 1997.

21 Encyclopedia Britannica, Inc: Encyclopedia Britannica Online, Chicago: "Eras in Black History." 2002.

22 AMEC Sunday School Union, Nashville, Tenn.: "The Doctrine and Discipline of the African Methodist Episcopal Church." 2000.

23 *Life Application Study Bible: King James Version*, Wheaton, Ill.: Tyndale House Publishers, Inc. 1997.

24 AMEC Sunday School Union, Nashville, Tenn.: "The Doctrine and Discipline of the African Methodist Episcopal Church." 2000.

25 Encyclopedia Britannica, Inc: Encyclopedia Britannica Online, Chicago: "Eras in Black History." 2002.

26 AMEC Sunday School Union, Nashville, Tenn.: "The Doctrine and Discipline of the African Methodist Episcopal Church." 2000.

27 Encyclopedia Britannica, Inc: Encyclopedia Britannica Online, Chicago: "Eras in Black History." 2002.

28 IAMG /Television Office of the University of Illinois-Springfield. Springfield, Ill.: "The IAMG Story." 1998.

29 AMEC Sunday School Union, Nashville, Tenn.: "The Doctrine and Discipline of the African Methodist Episcopal Church." 2000.

30 IAMG /Television Office of the University of Illinois-Springfield. Springfield, Ill.: "The IAMG Story." 1998.

31 Encyclopedia Britannica, Inc: Encyclopedia Britannica Online, Chicago: "Eras in Black History." 2002.

32 Substance of Hope, Indianapolis: "Substance of Hope Committee Vision & Mission." 1998.

33 Bethel African Methodist Episcopal Church, Indianapolis: "A brief history of Bethel African Methodist Episcopal Church, Indianapolis, Ind." 2002. Frances C. Stout.

34 Encyclopedia Britannica, Inc: Encyclopedia Britannica Online, Chicago: "Eras in Black History." 2002.